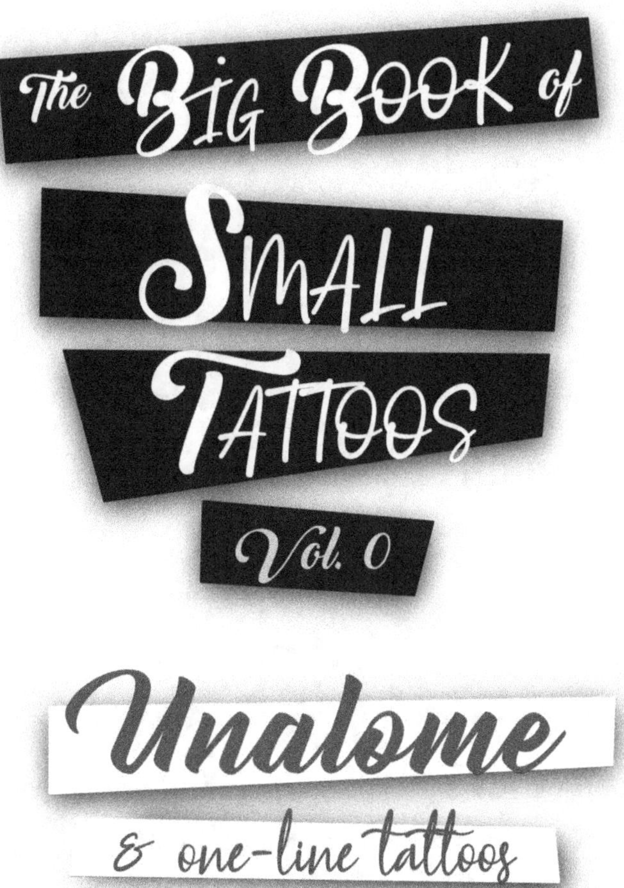

The Big Book of Small Tattoos

Vol. 0

Unalome

& one-line tattoos

TattooTribes

2021

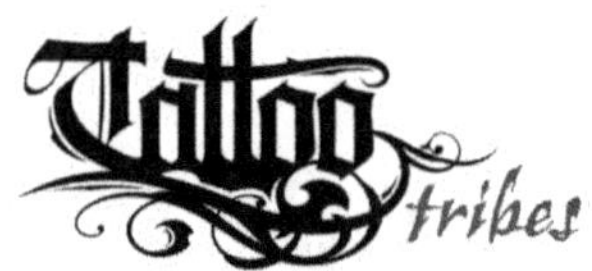

TattooTribes Ed.

© 2021 Roberto Gemori.

Contents

This is a monographic volume entirely dedicated to unalomes and unalome-inspired designs.

Enjoy

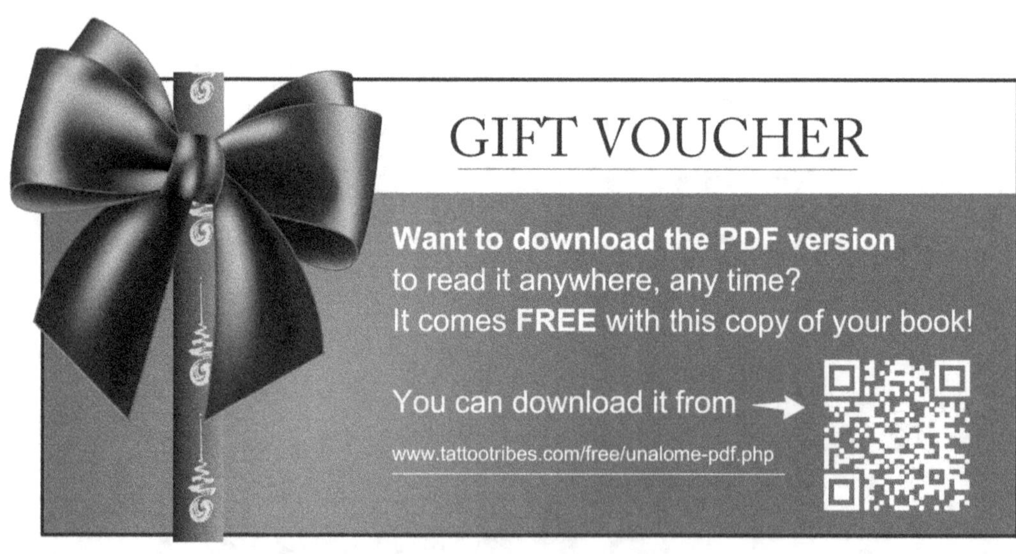
GIFT VOUCHER

Want to download the PDF version
to read it anywhere, any time?
It comes FREE with this copy of your book!

You can download it from →

www.tattootribes.com/free/unalome-pdf.php

Preface

Unalome tattoos have gained great popularity over the last years, but **what exactly are unalomes? What do they represent? Is it right for you to get one? What is the best placement?**
This book answers these questions and features 100+ original, unpublished unalome-inspired designs to give you ideas for a small personal tattoo that really speaks to you if you decide you want one.
The book is divided into four parts:

- Origin, meaning, and description of the unalome symbol

- Traditional design examples

- Modern unalome designs

- One-liners, or simple designs shaped by a single continuous line, for those who love the look of unalomes but don't feel committed to their symbolism

Wondering why "Vol. 0"?

That's not a mistake: we used zero because even if this book belongs to a series dedicated to small tattoos, it's actually an independent book on unalomes in its own right.
THE book on unalomes!

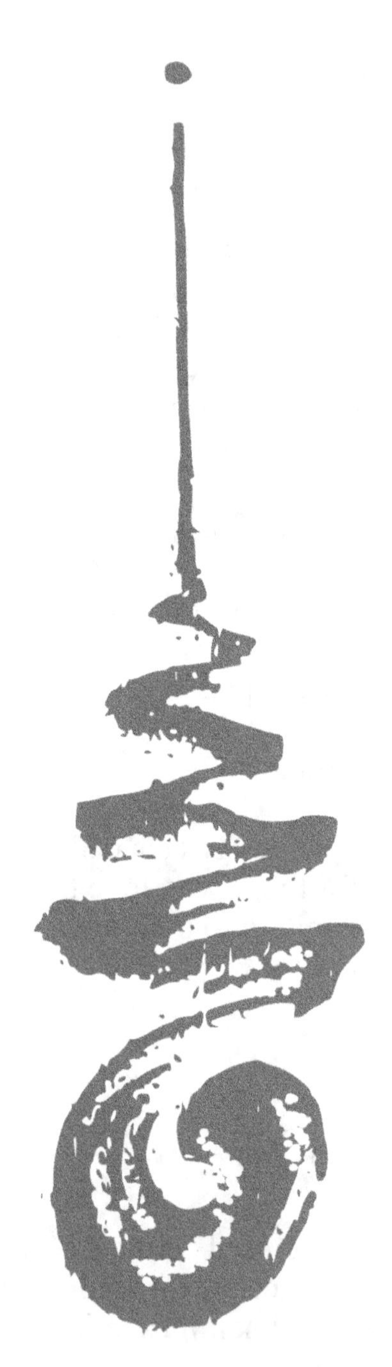

What is an unalome?

Both the representation and the symbolism of the unalome share many similarities to the right-turning conch shell design, one of the eight auspicious Buddhist symbols. The white conch shell represents the supremacy of the Buddha's teachings, the thoughts of the Buddha, and it may have actually been the inspiration for the unalome itself.

While the conch shell is more common in artwork, unalomes have become popular in Sak Yant tattoos, which are tattoos based on ancient Indic *yantras* (or *yant*).

To quickly explain what a *yantra* is, let's reference a similar word you probably already know: *mantra*. A *mantra* is a sacred syllable, a short sound that carries a spiritual power, repeated in religious rituals and meditative practices to cultivate a higher state of consciousness.

A *yantra* is its visual counterpart: they are geometrical diagrams used as magic charms to support *mantras*, with both psychological and spiritual power. While *mantras* work with sounds, *yantras* are graphical.

Complex Sak Yant tattoos embody the essence of their bearer's own identity, and often operate to attract mundane results (namely riches, health, appeal, and so on).

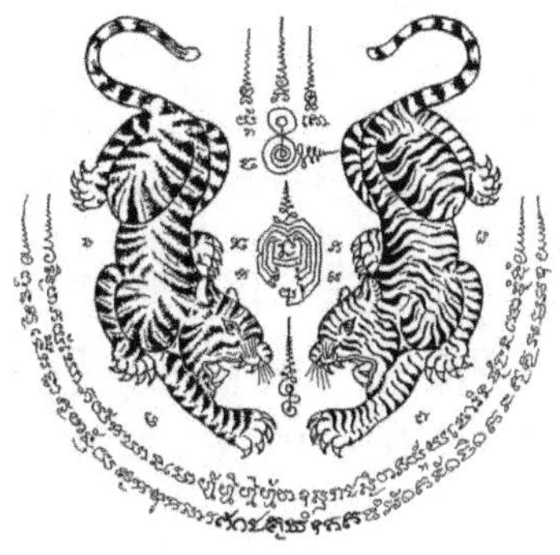

Yant Suea Koo
leader, fearless, power over the others

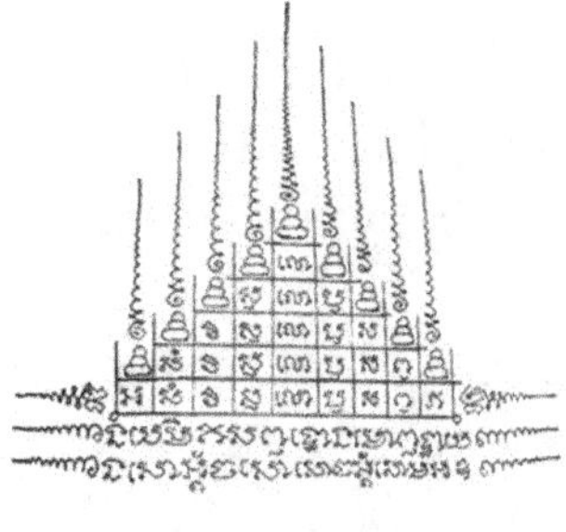

Yant Gao Yord
protection, avoid danger and harms

Na Yant, or small *yantras*, often based on syllables of the Khmer alphabet, remain closer to the original Buddhist teachings and often relate to spiritual qualities instead. The unalome belongs to this last group.

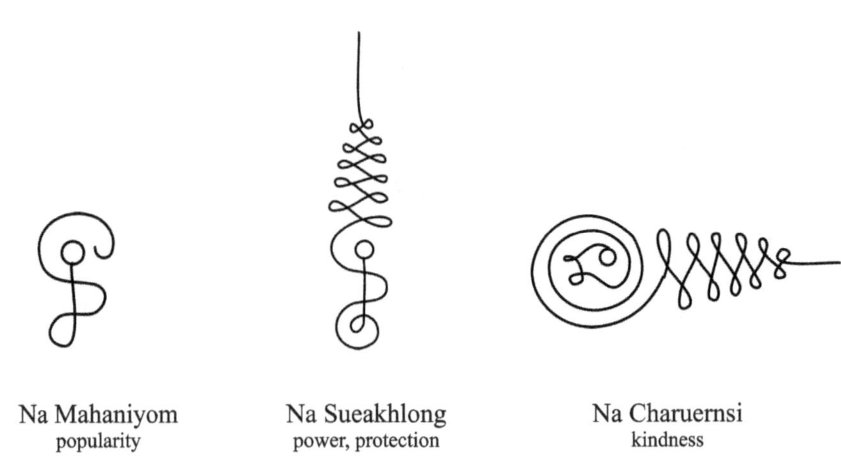

Na Mahaniyom
popularity

Na Sueakhlong
power, protection

Na Charuernsi
kindness

Like many Na Yant, the unalome is believed to mobilize energy, hiding a deep meaning behind its visual simplicity.

Here possibly lies the greatest appeal of this symbol: we see complexity all around us in everyday life and modern society, and we deeply strive to find our way through it, to bring everything down to simplicity in an attempt to reach our inner north, a meaning and a purpose to our own lives.

That's exactly what the unalome teaches, and it does it in the simplest way, with a single line, because simplicity is key to its symbolism.

We can identify three main parts of the unalome: a spiral, a wandering path, and a straight path. It's not uncommon to see a separate dot at the end.

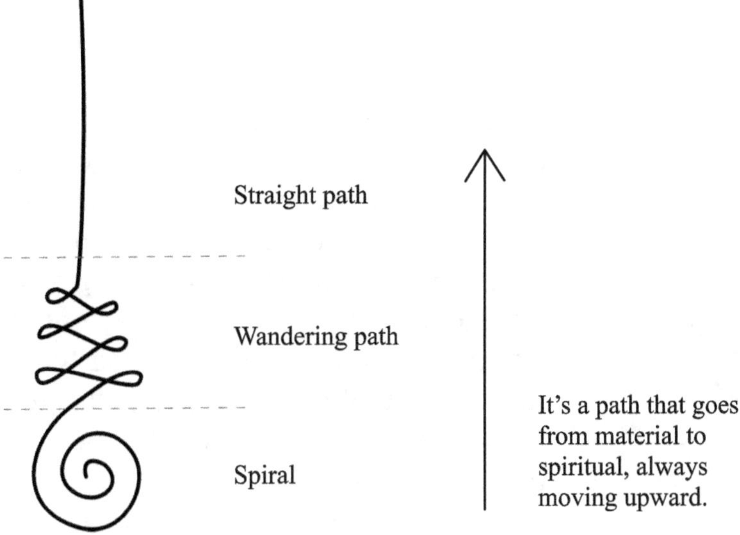

Each part carries a different significance and together they represent the path of personal growth toward spiritual enlightenment.

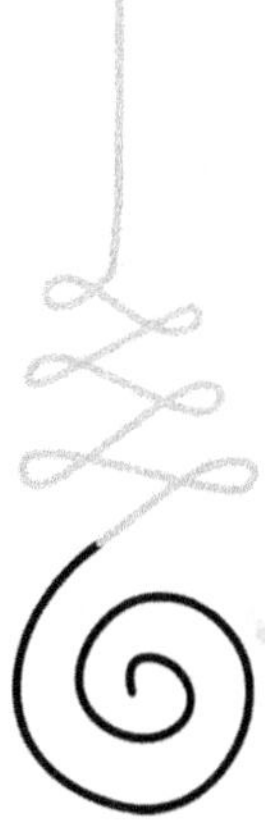

The center of the spiral represents birth, our beginning in life. The spiral itself represents our life going through several incarnations, as we are prone to repeat the same mistakes over and over again, yet learning from them and widening our perspective and consciousness until we successfully break free from this cycle to really start our personal journey.

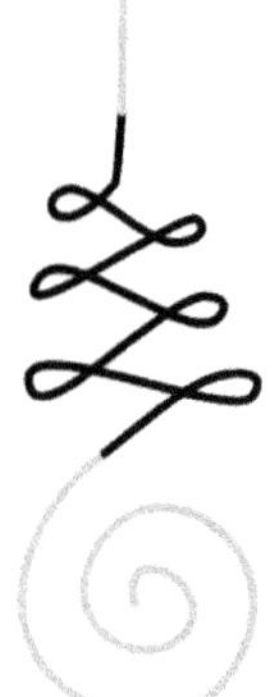

This section corresponds to the second part of our journey, where we wander and move forward by trial and error, and by gaining more experience every time.

Even when the path seems to go ahead, we sometimes fall back. Learning from this can help us avoid repeating the same mistakes, making them less frequently, and eventually proceeding more and more consciously ahead, with every knot symbolizing a spiritual milestone.

Each individual will have a uniquely different path as there are not two identical persons who will share an exactly identical story. Each of us will have to find their own path to fulfill their true potential.

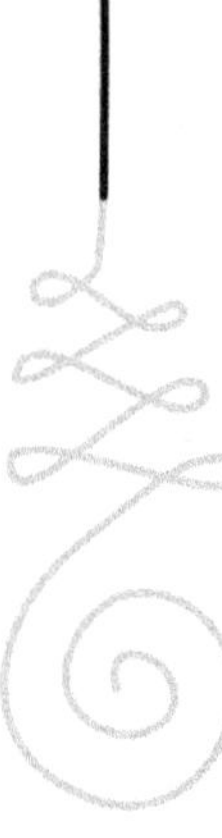

The straight line at the end of the unalome represents when we finally find our path and follow it unwaveringly.

A dot, if present, symbolizes perfection, enlightenment. It is separated from the path because, according to the teaching of the Buddha, only by leaving material ties and pleasures behind us can we reach it.

Another interpretation suggests that the dot represents our true purpose in life, and the path to achieve it puts us to a test that challenges our spirit and fortifies it so that we can finally fulfill our true potential.

Orientation and masculine/feminine energy

The orientation of the spiral is sometimes associated with masculine or feminine energy. While we can't be sure it was originally so, it's a possibility that we should not dismiss if we consider the conch shell to be the origin of the unalome symbol.

The conch shell has a spiraling shape that ends with an opening on one end and a point on the other. From its point, the spiral can expand in a clockwise (left-turning) or counterclockwise (right-turning) direction. The latter is rarer and therefore auspicious.

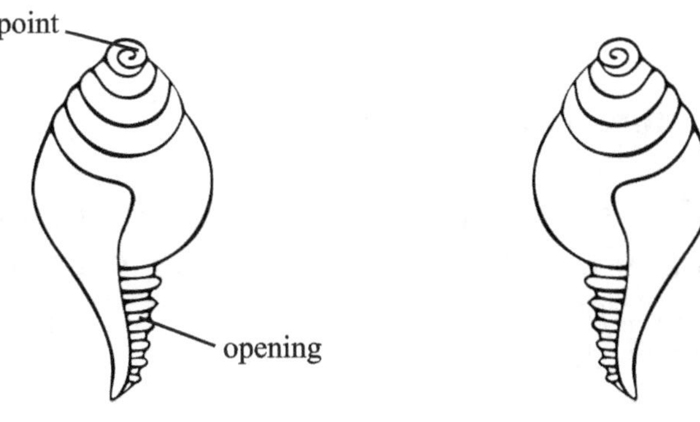

Right-turning shell   Left-turning shell

Looking at the shell from the side of the point (which makes it look similar to the unalome representation), the direction and symbolism of the unalome spiral duplicates the direction and symbolism of the conch shell:

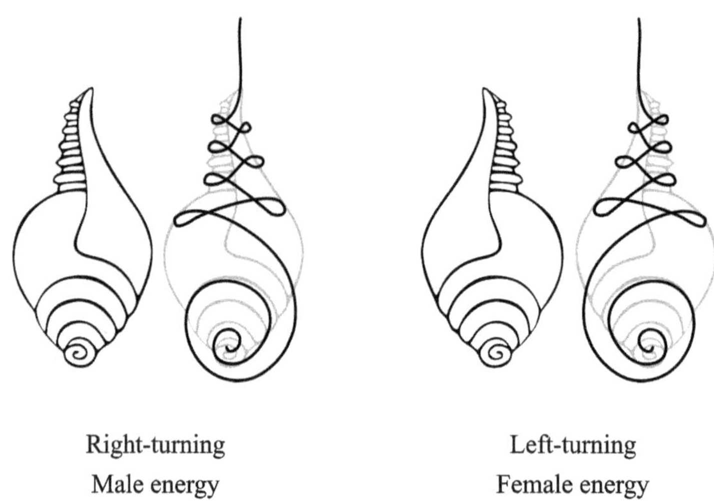

Right-turning
Male energy

Left-turning
Female energy

Based on the tradition that associates the left with female energy and the right with male, the orientation of the spiral is associated with feminine or masculine energy accordingly.

Important note about positioning

If you wish to get a unalome tattoo without being disrespectful of the religion it comes from, consider placing it higher than your waist. All that is lower, closer to the soil, is considered earth-bound and impure.

Placing it on the foot, for example, would be considered highly disrespectful, whereas the ideal positioning would be on a higher *chakra* (*chakra* means *"wheel, whirl"*, these are energy points in our body), with the straight line pointing upward.

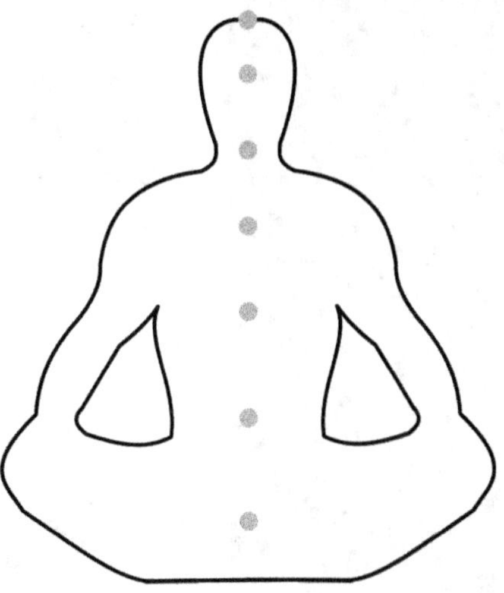

Quick note on the style

All designs will be presented in the simplest possible way, with a single, clean black line. Of course, they can be inked in color, shadowed, done with paintbrush-like strokes and in any other way that will make your unalome one of a kind.
Make it *yours*!

Traditional designs

The unalome design will always include the spiral, the wandering path, and the straight path. The dot can be present or not.

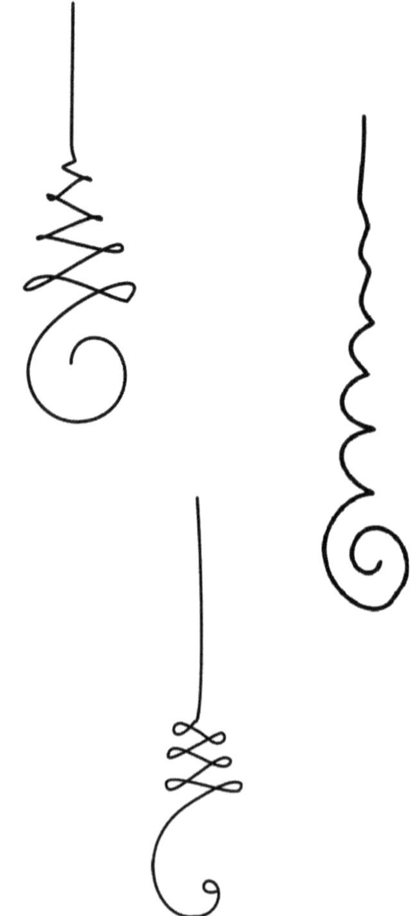

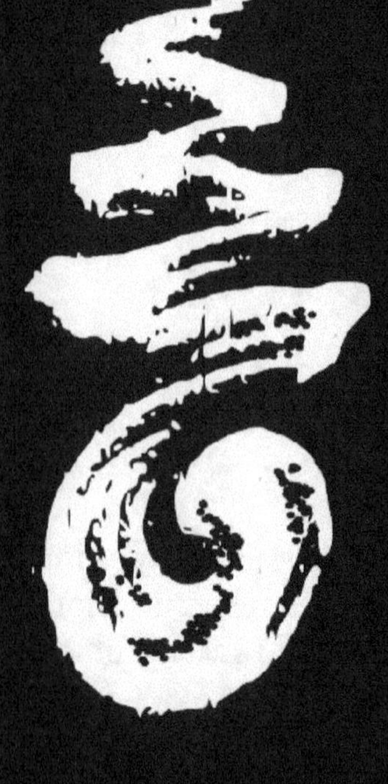

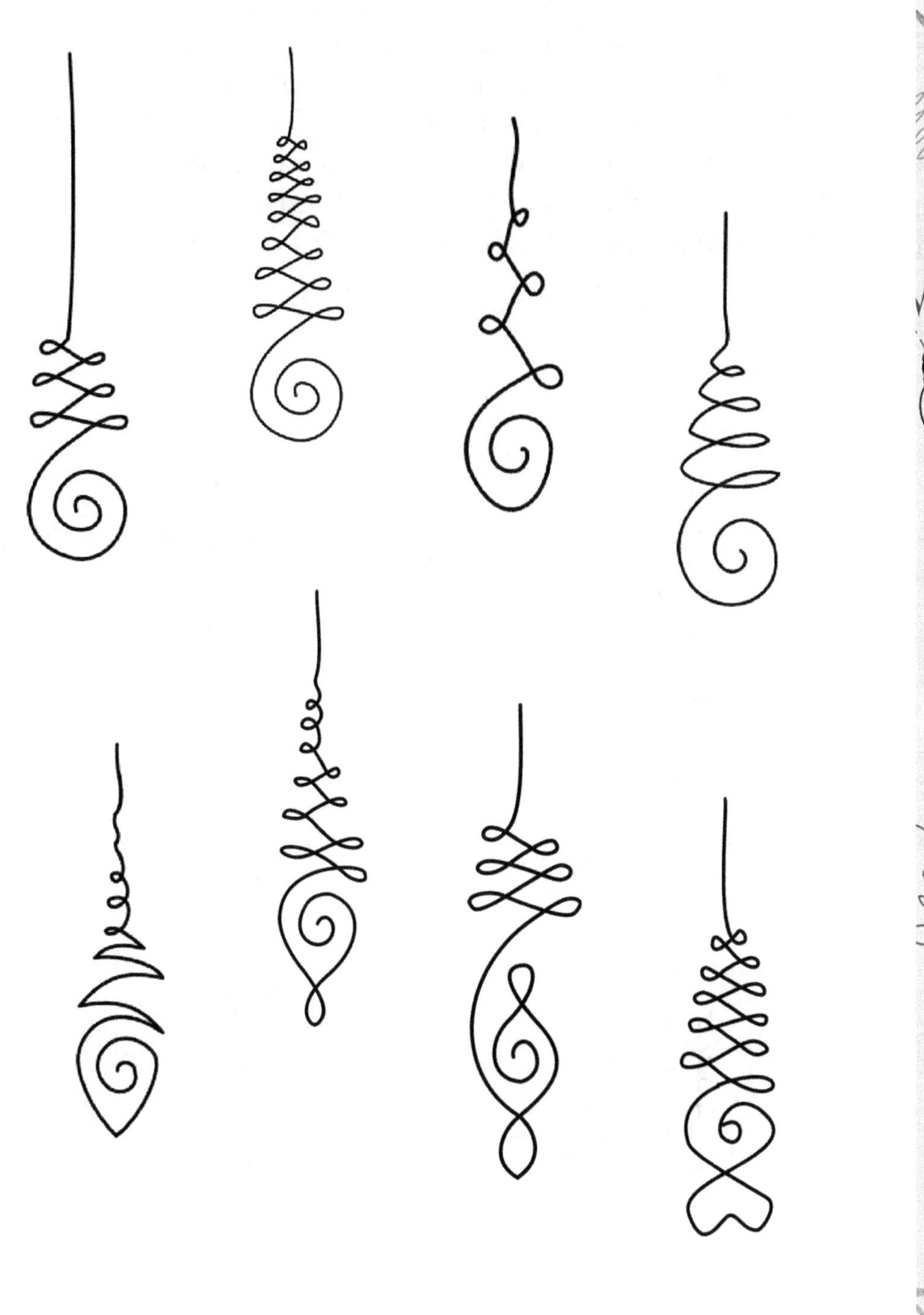

There are several Na Yant tattoos like the unalome that include Khmer syllables instead of having the spiral.

Since each syllable can have several different meanings and act in several different ways as a sacred *yantra*, you should talk to a traditional practitioner before getting any of them inked as they require specific ceremonies to be activated correctly. Some of them are shown below for illustration purposes.

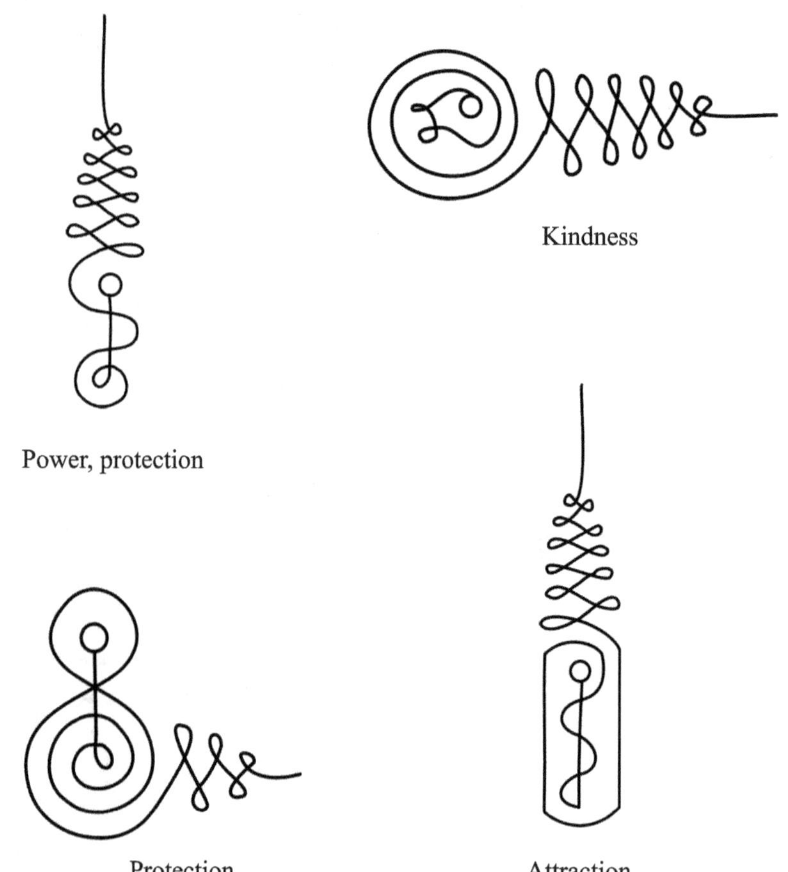

Power, protection

Kindness

Protection

Attraction

Traditional designs

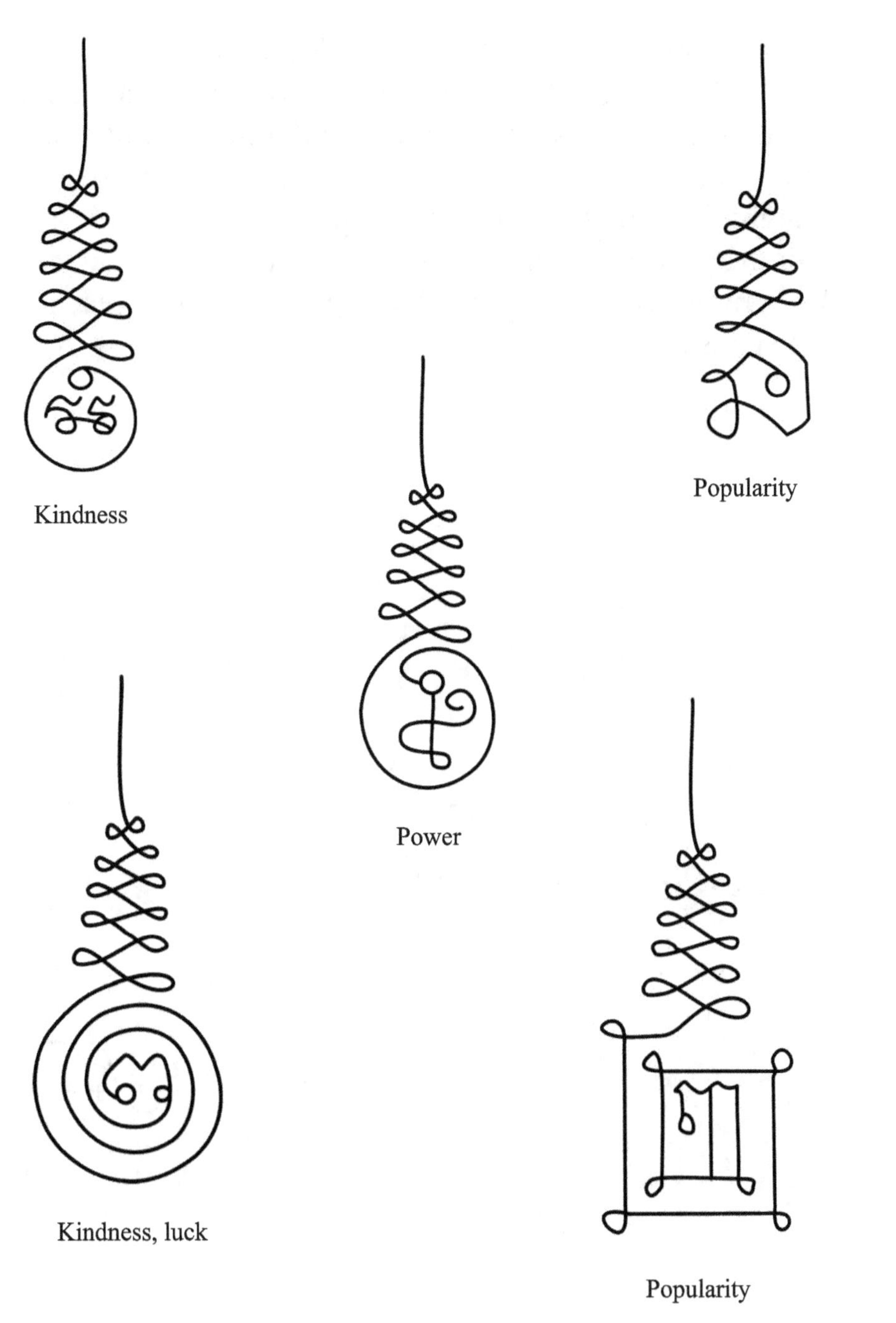

Kindness

Popularity

Power

Kindness, luck

Popularity

Unalomes also appear in Sak Yant tattoos next to other elements, where they can also signify arahants (enlightened saints), with the spiral representing their crown and the straight line representing their path to enlightenment, which they accomplished.

In the Yant Gao Yord tattoo below, nine unalomes can be seen above the nine meditating arahants who reached the status of Buddha.

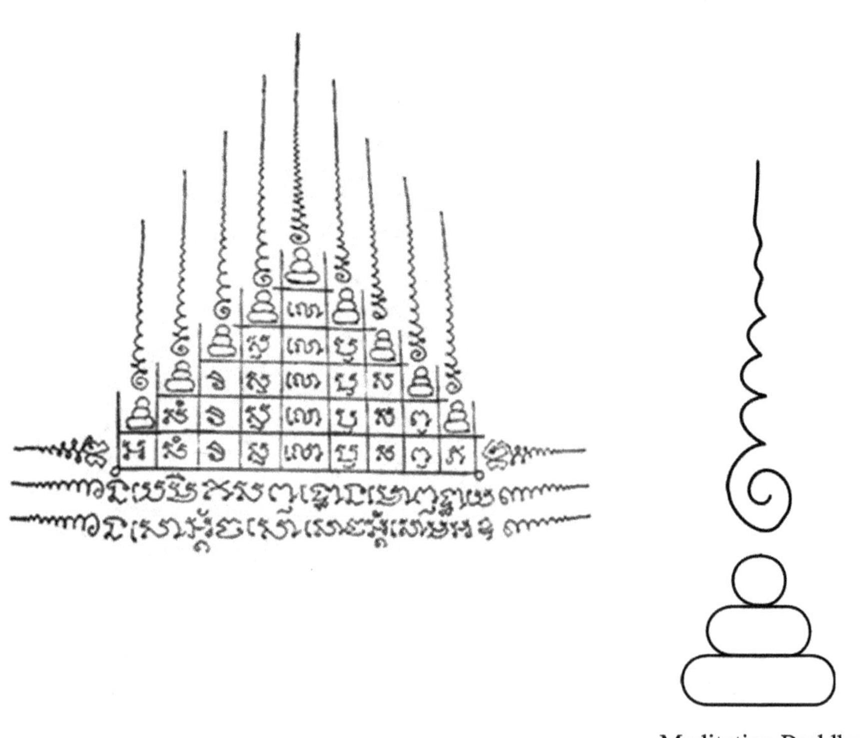

Meditating Buddha

Other symbols that often appear in association with the unalome, and which will take the stage in the next chapter, are the lotus flower, the moon, and the sun.

The lotus flower

The lotus flower symbolizes overcoming adversities, as it blooms immaculate and pure above the muddy waters it is born in. It's a metaphor of human life and of the struggle to break free from material matters in order to achieve a higher knowledge.

The moon

The moon is a symbol of femininity and fertility. In Buddhism it is also considered a symbol of light in the darkness, and it metaphorically symbolizes knowledge bringing light through the darkness of ignorance.

The sun

The sun is a symbol of masculinity and eternity, also used to symbolize the victory of life over death. It is related to fire, which is a symbol of wisdom incinerating the five poisons of ignorance, desire, aversion, pride, and jealousy.

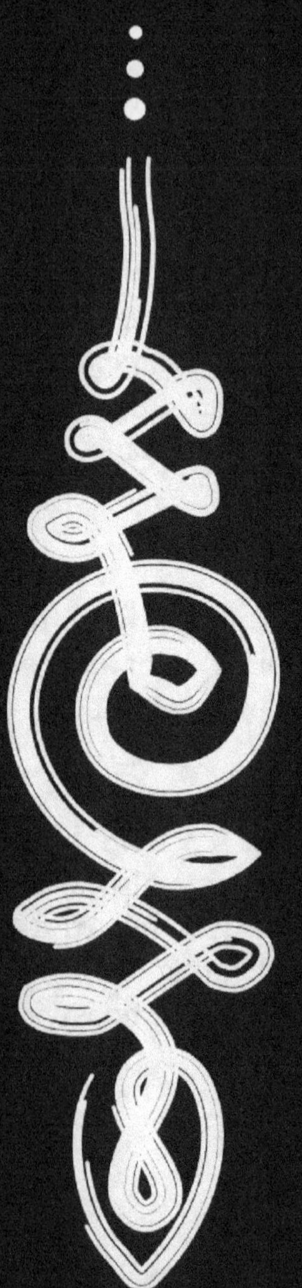

This chapter features designs that keep the unalome as their base and expand it or blend it with other traditional symbols like the lotus flower, the moon, the sun, and more.

Following the concept of Na Yant incorporating syllables, one section is dedicated to unalomes incorporating Latin letters.

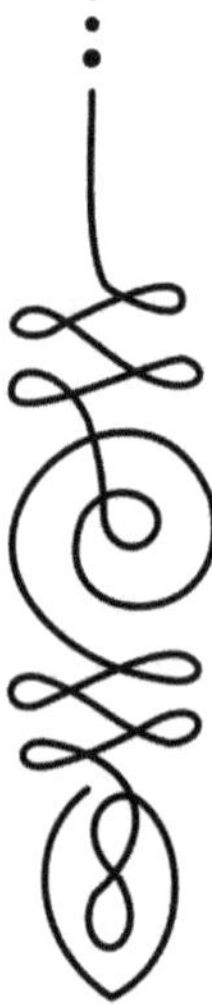

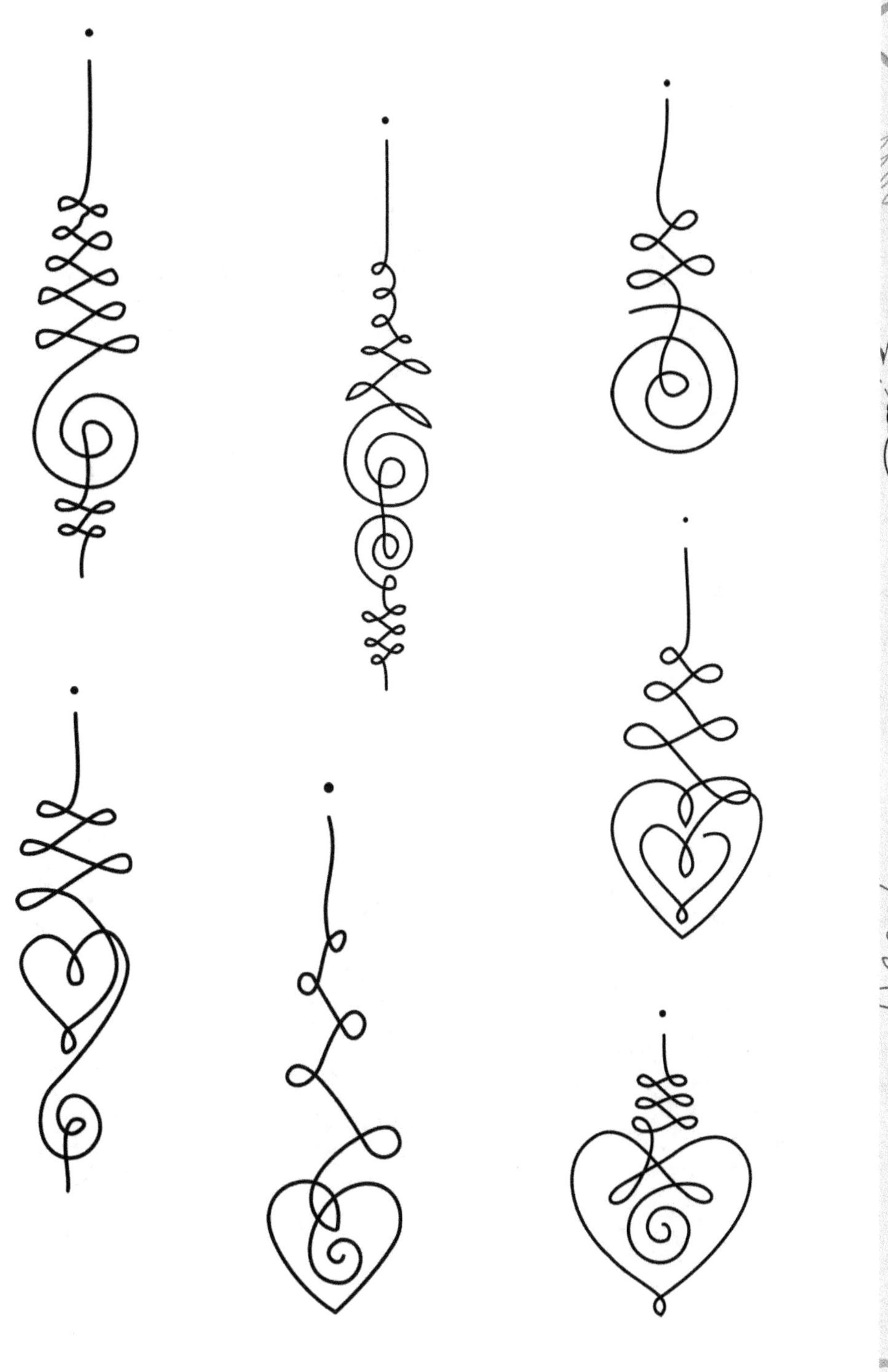

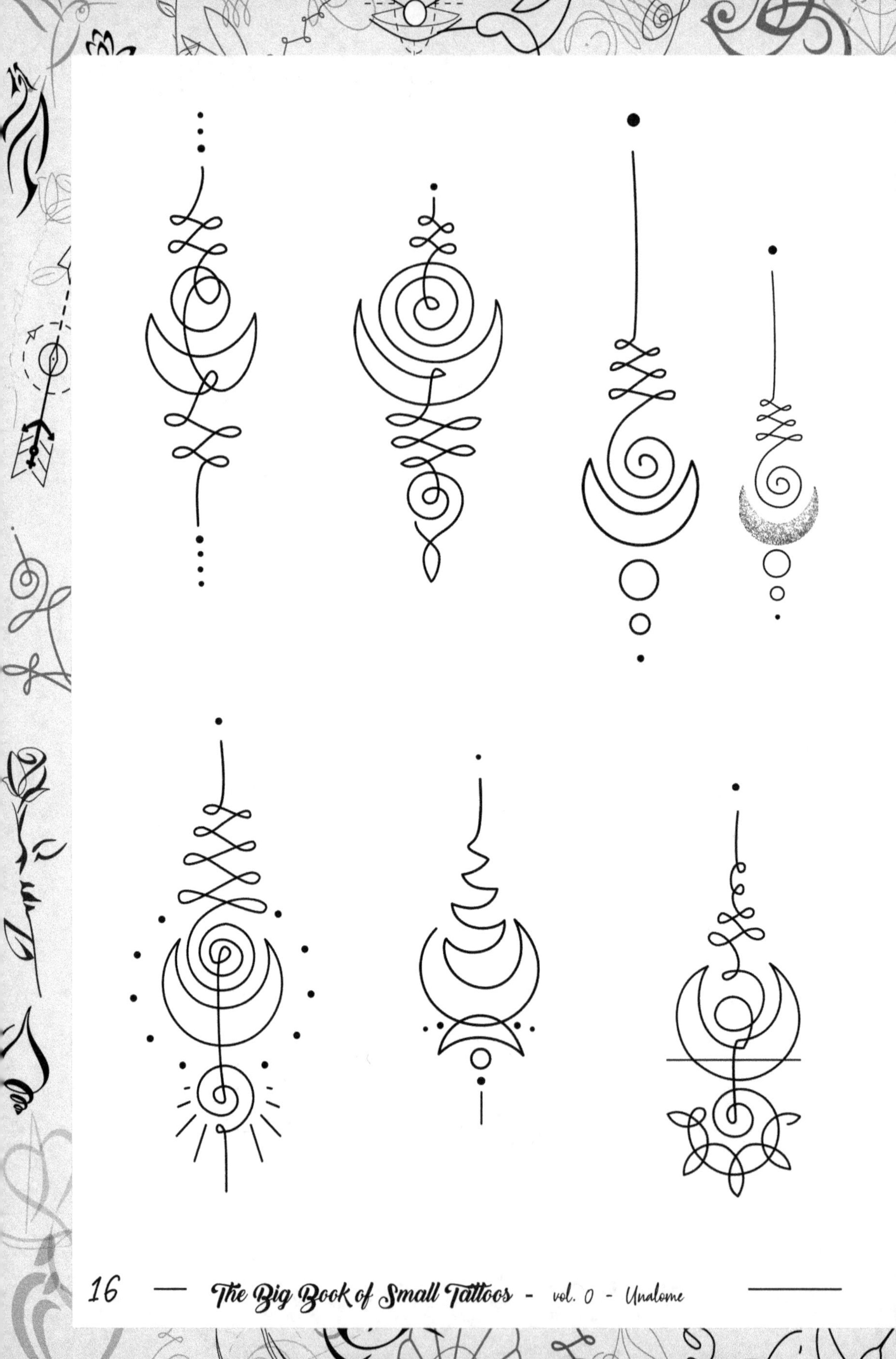

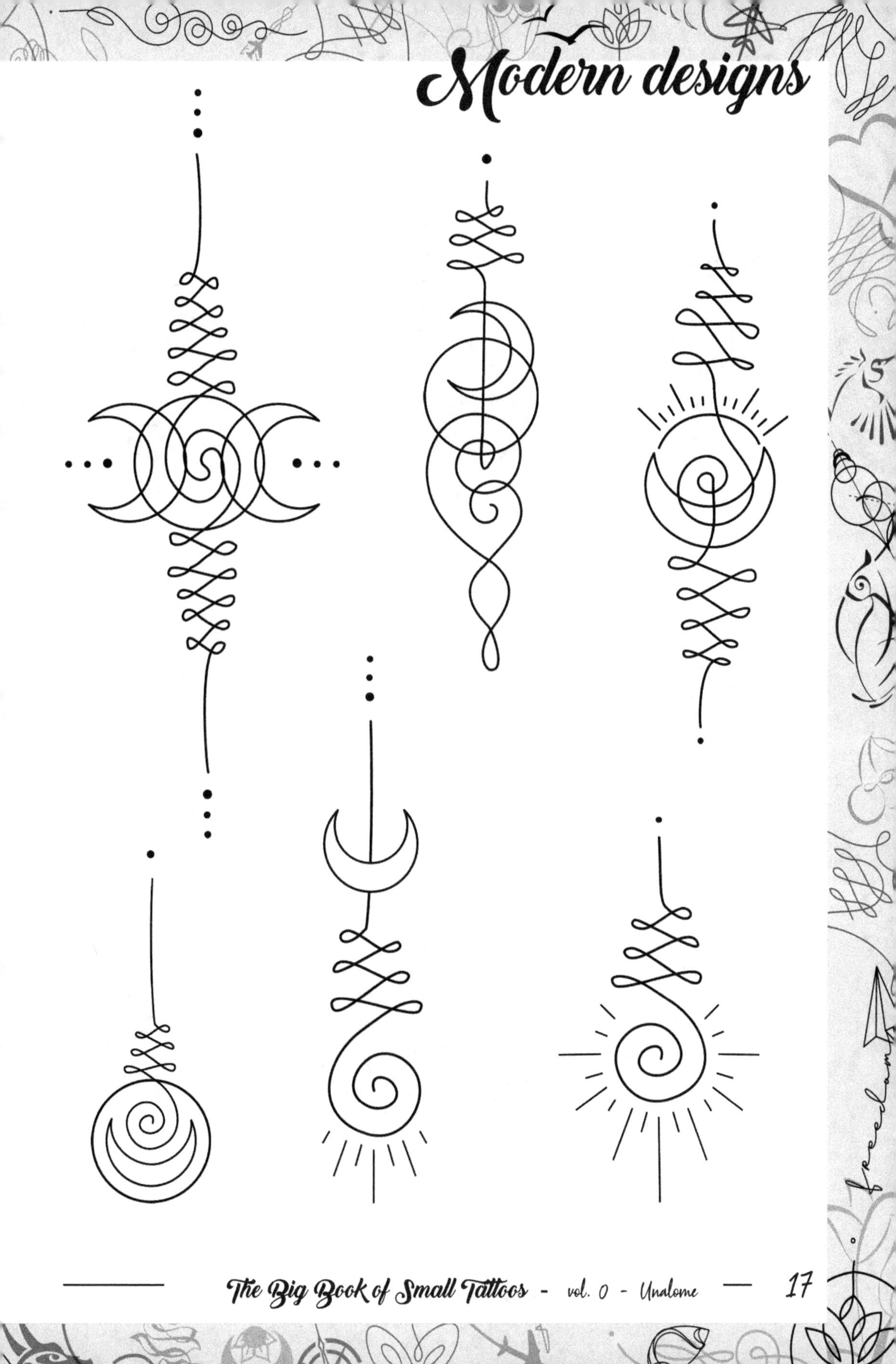

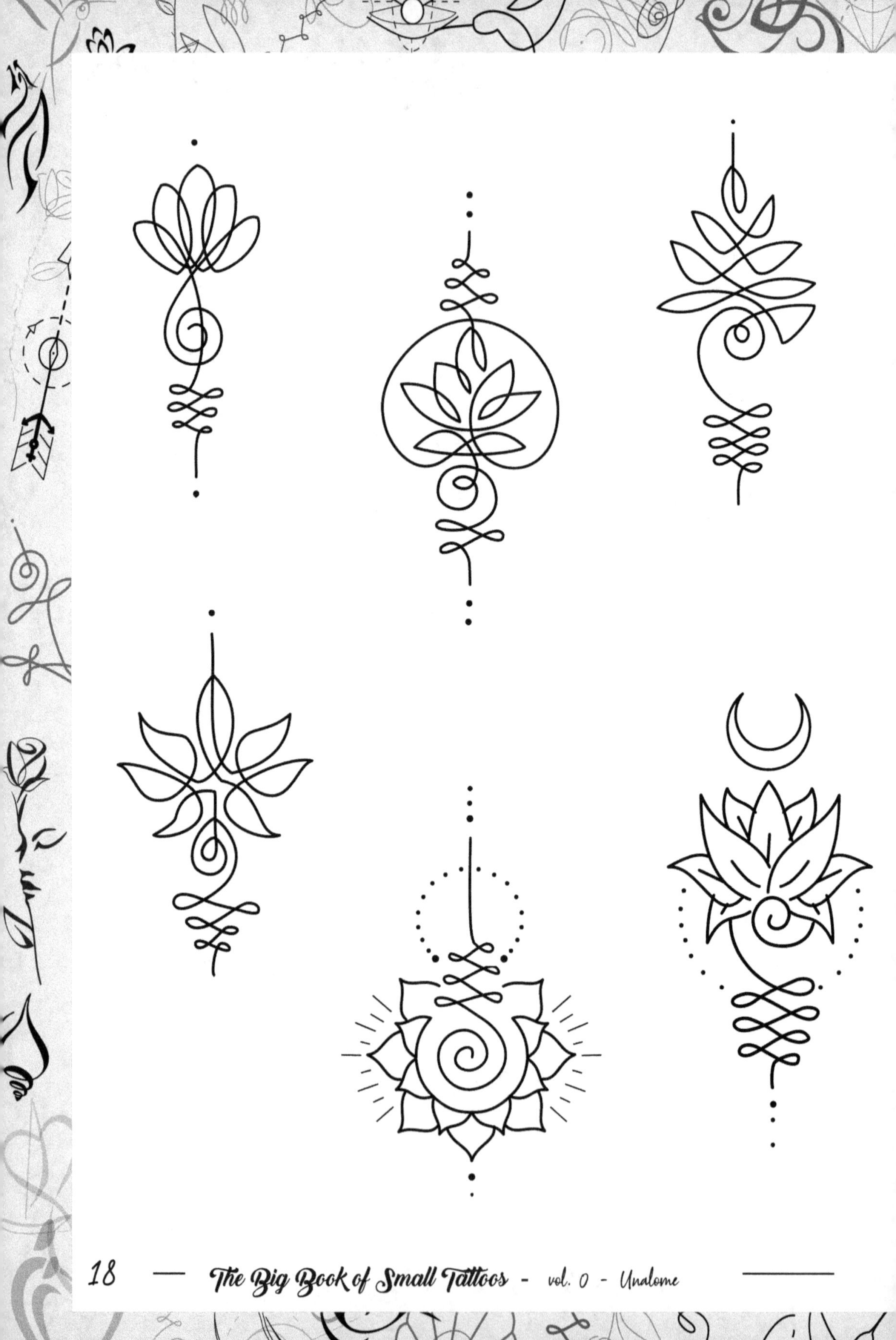

Modern designs

— A —

— B —

— C —

— D —

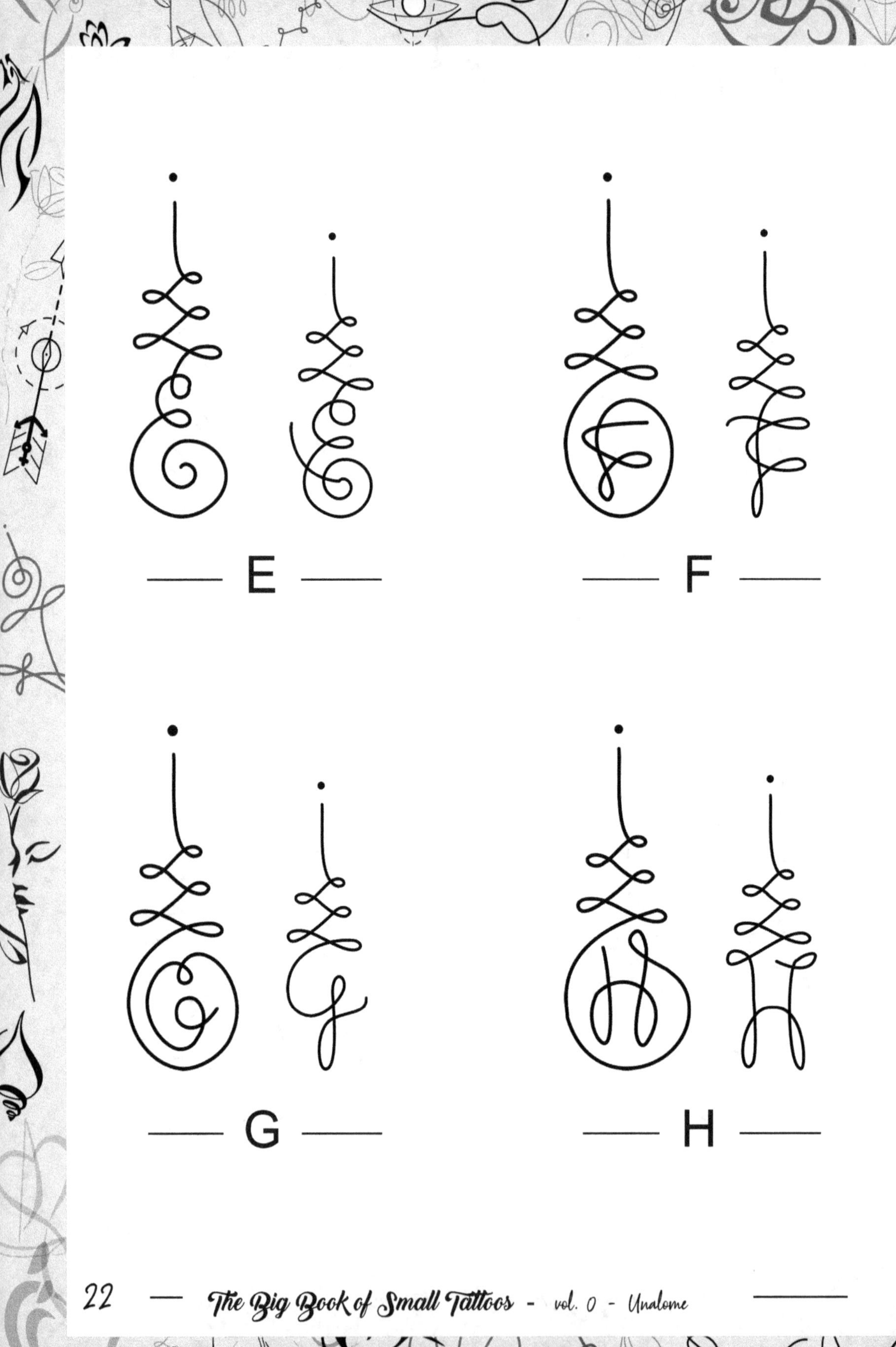
E
F
G
H

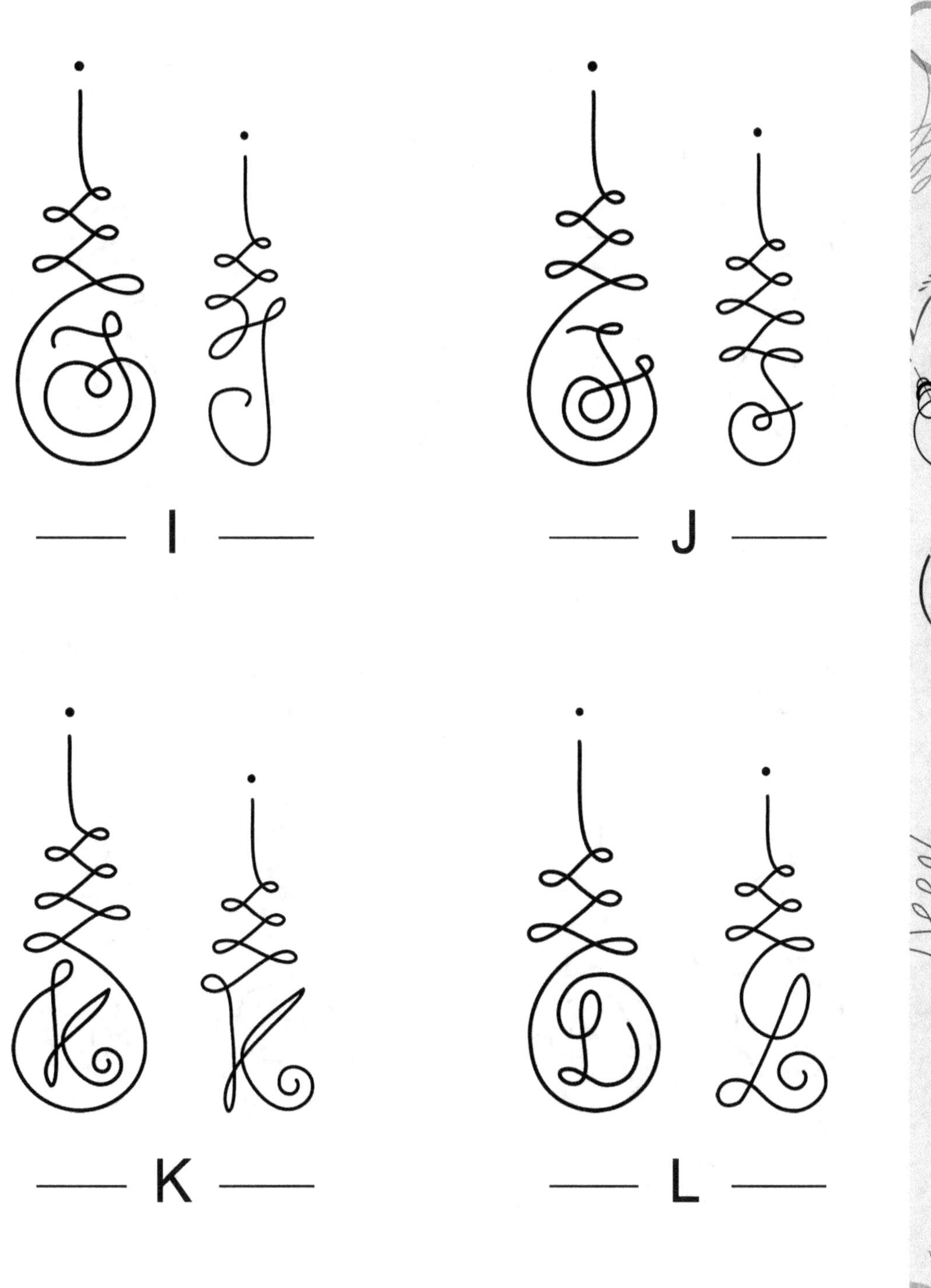

I
J
K
L

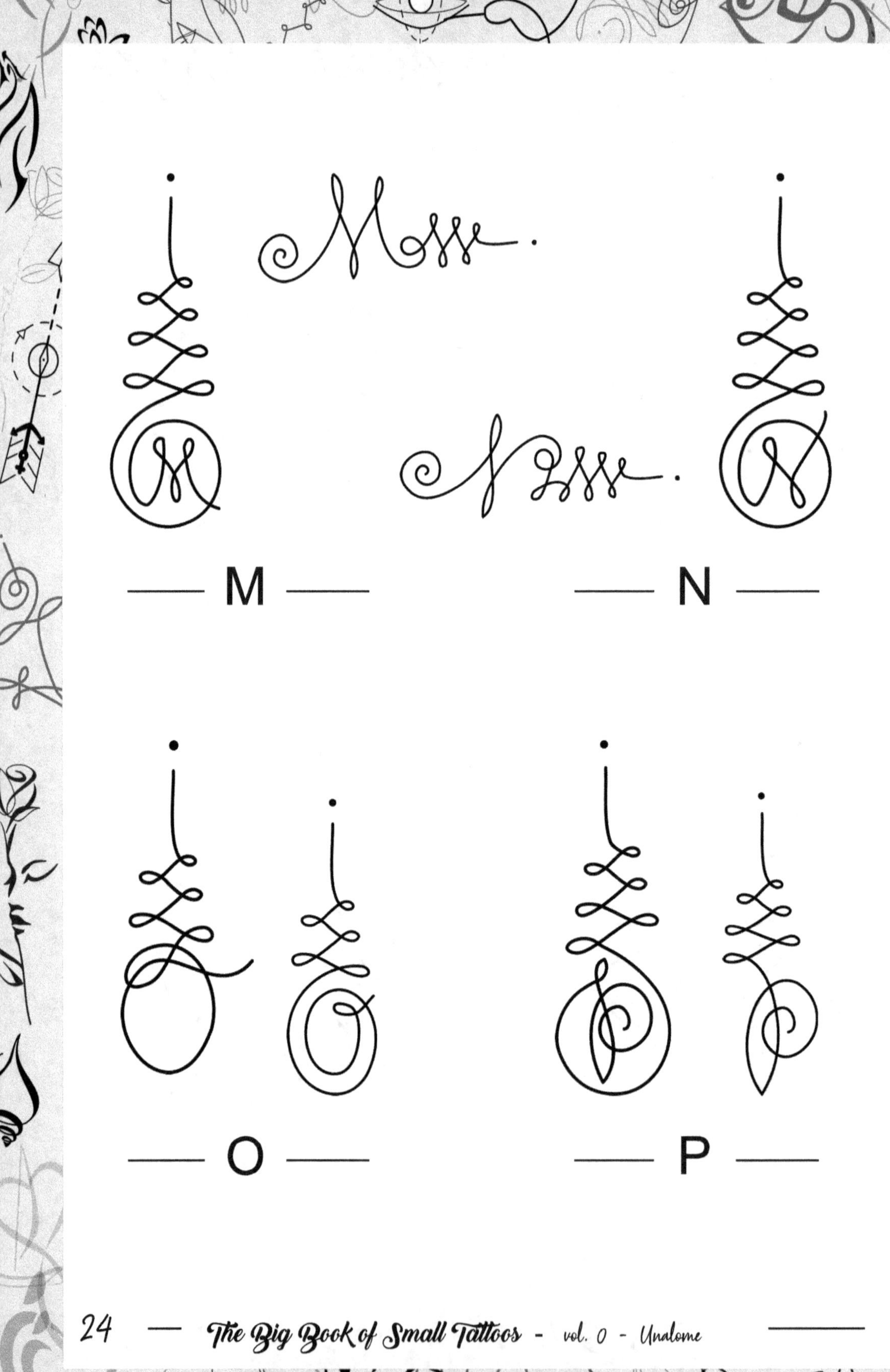

M
N
O
P

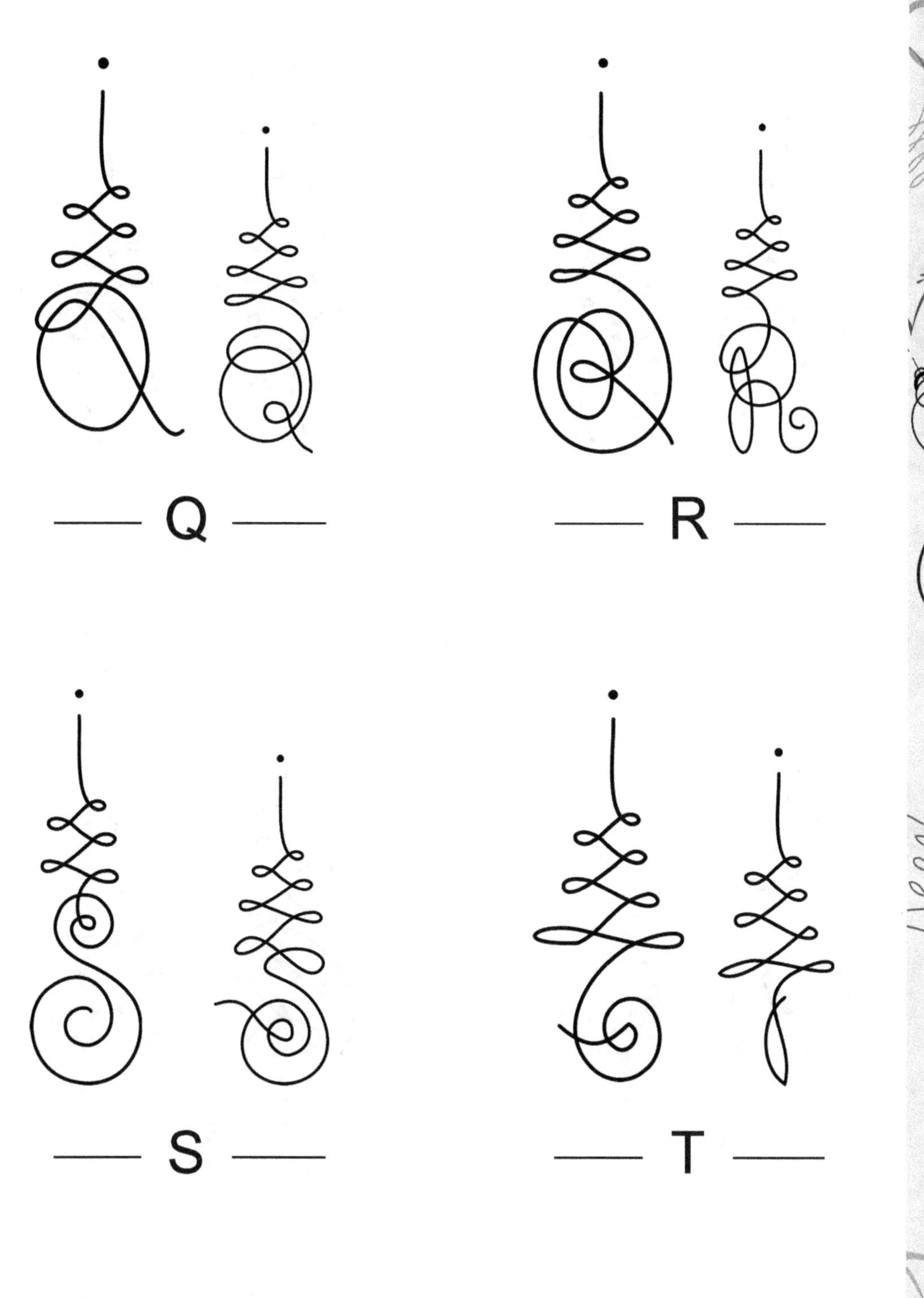

Q
R
S
T

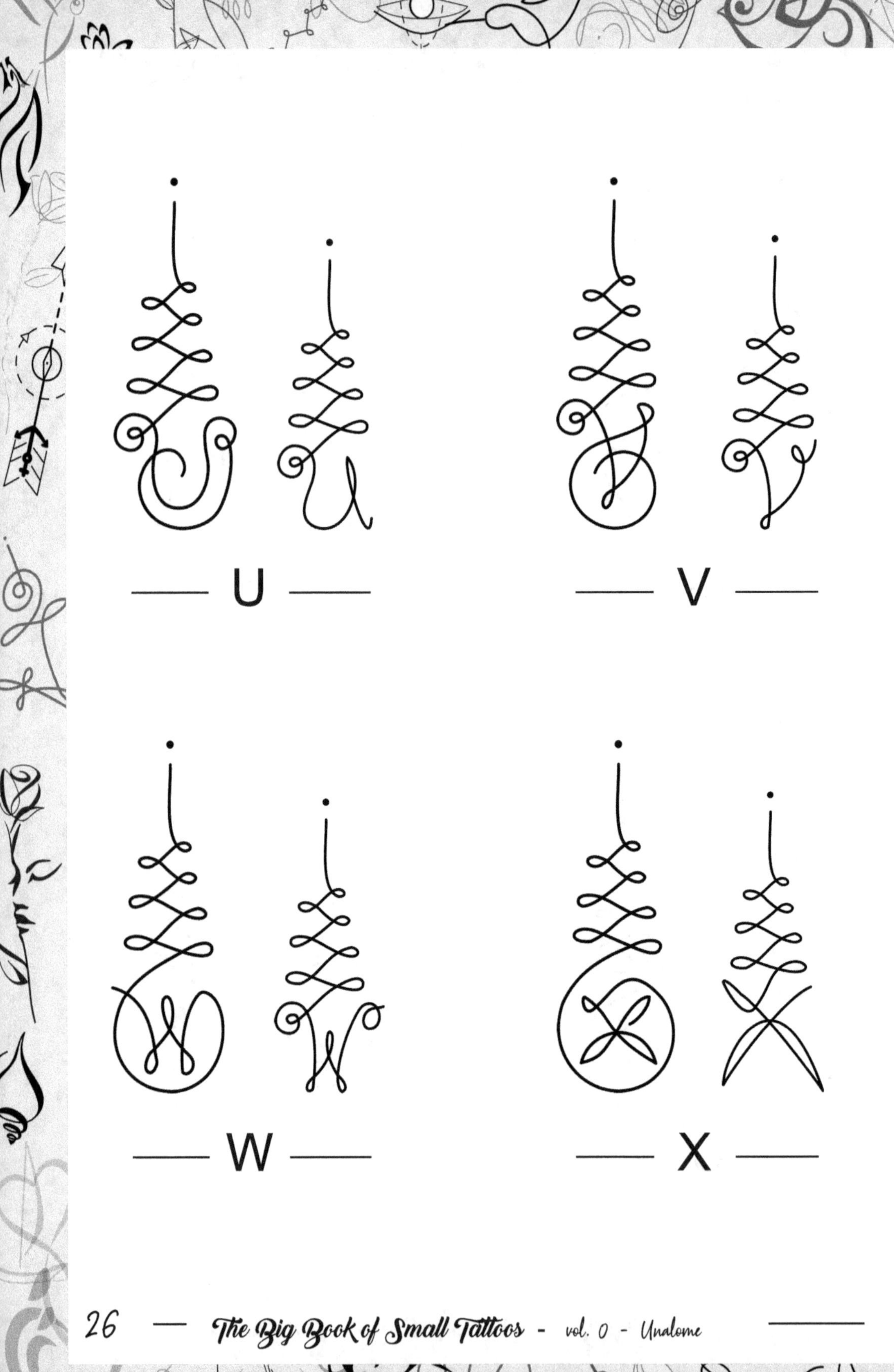

— U —

— V —

— W —

— X —

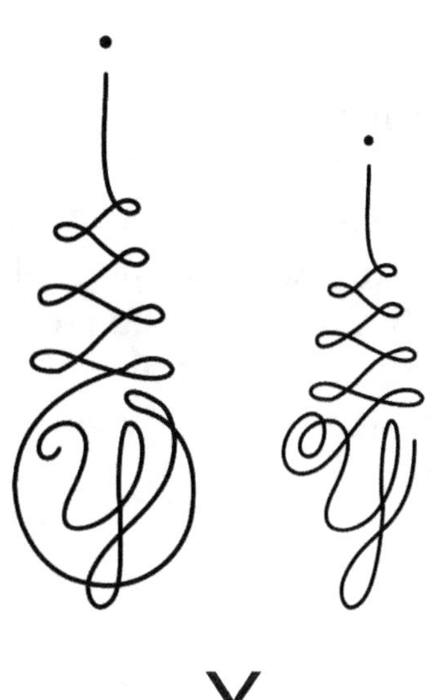

— Y —

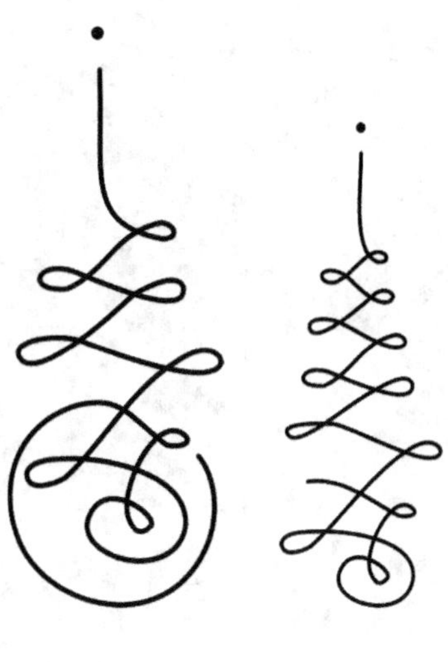

— Z —

Of course, letter unalomes can be paired with other symbols and elements to customize them and make them more meaningful to you.

Your baby girl's name starts with S and you want to celebrate her birth? Here's a quick example of a possible way to do it, adding a moon and a small pacifier to the S unalome:

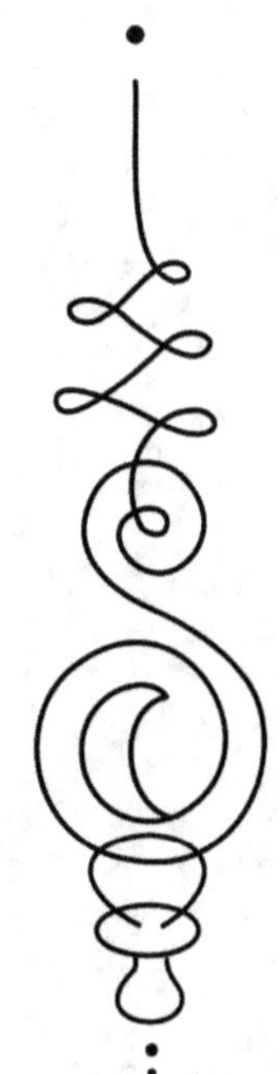

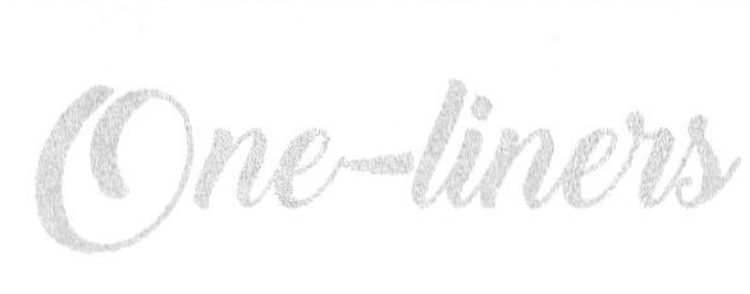

One-liners

As the name says, one-liners are drawings made by a single continuous line. Some of the designs in this chapter still share traits of the unalome and include the spiral and the wandering path whenever possible.

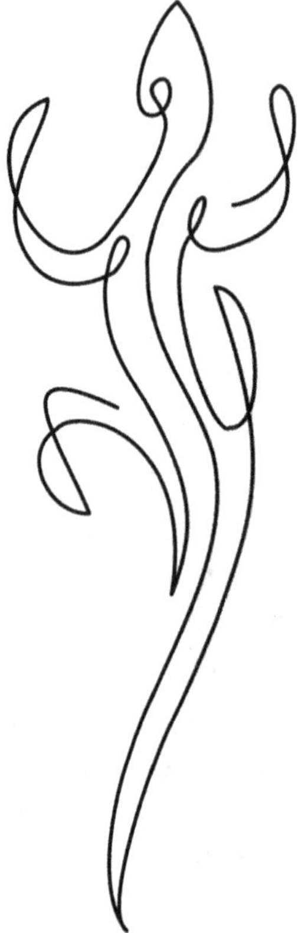

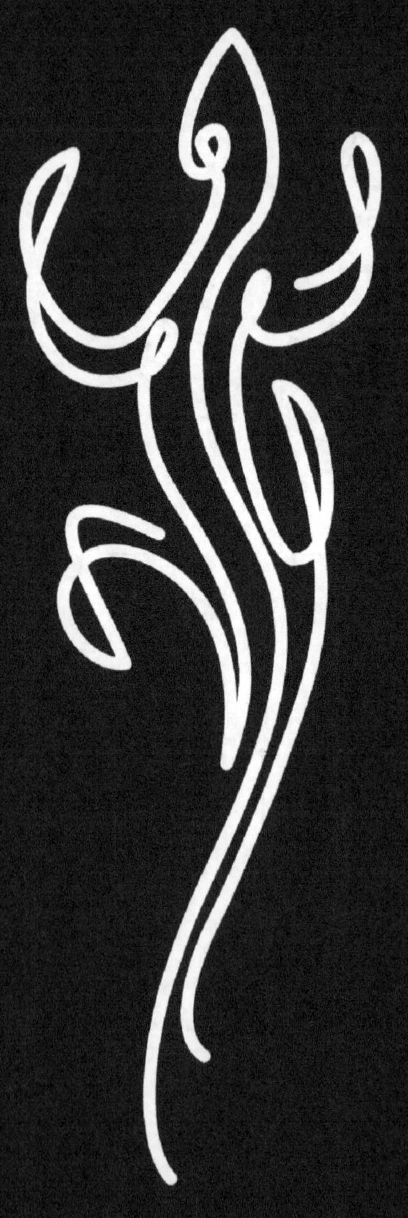

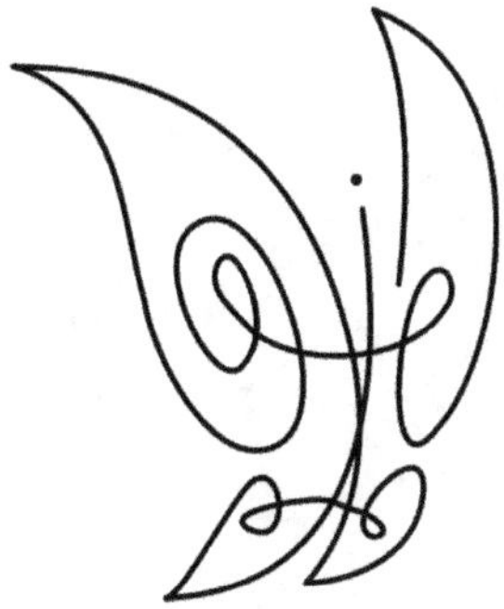

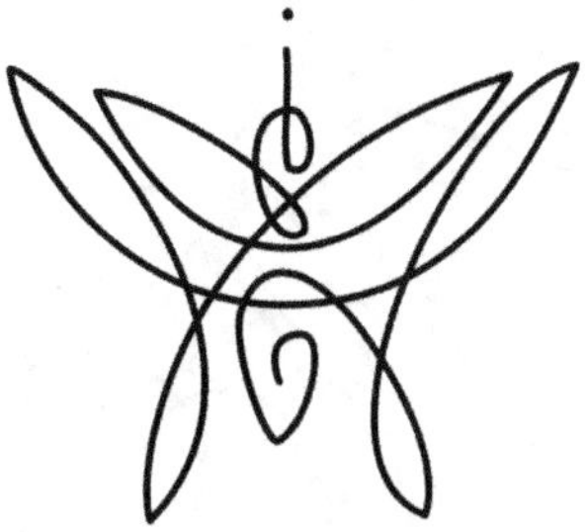

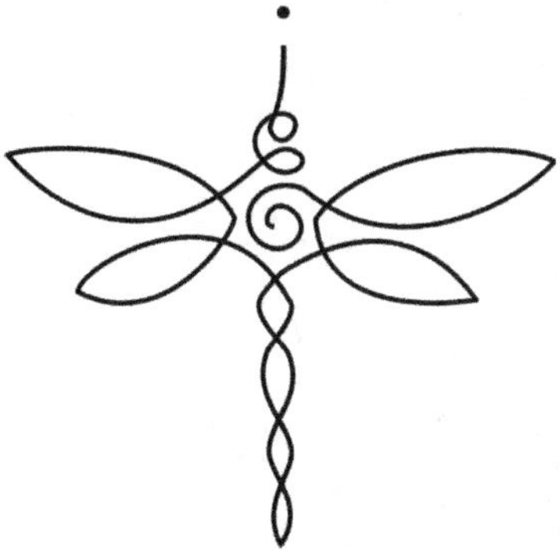

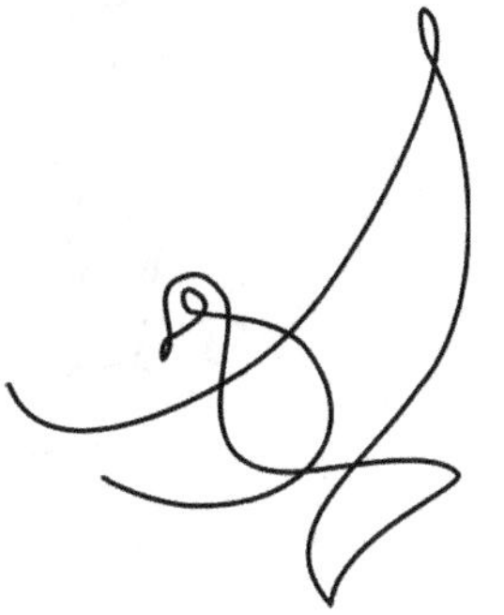

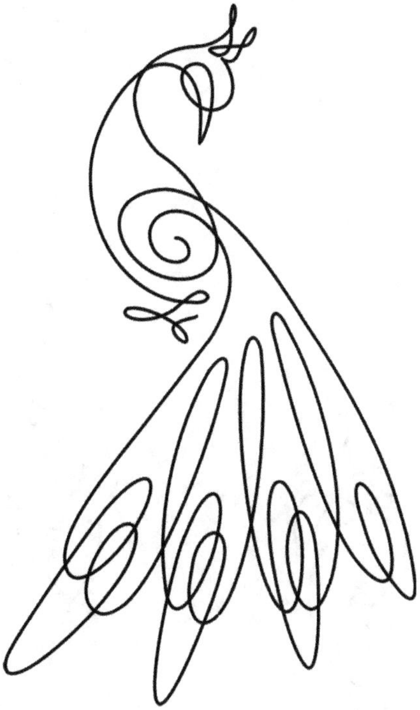

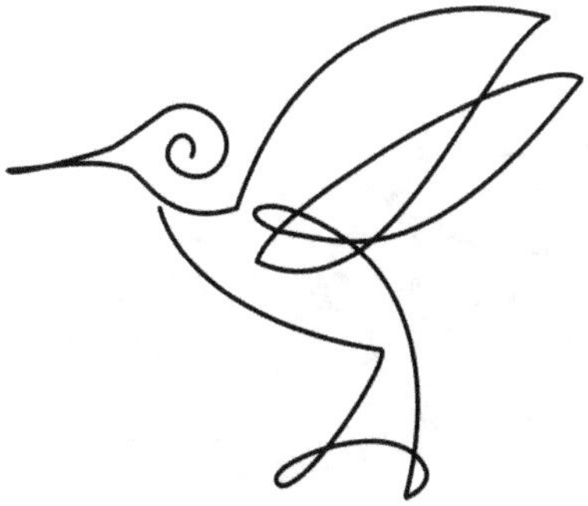

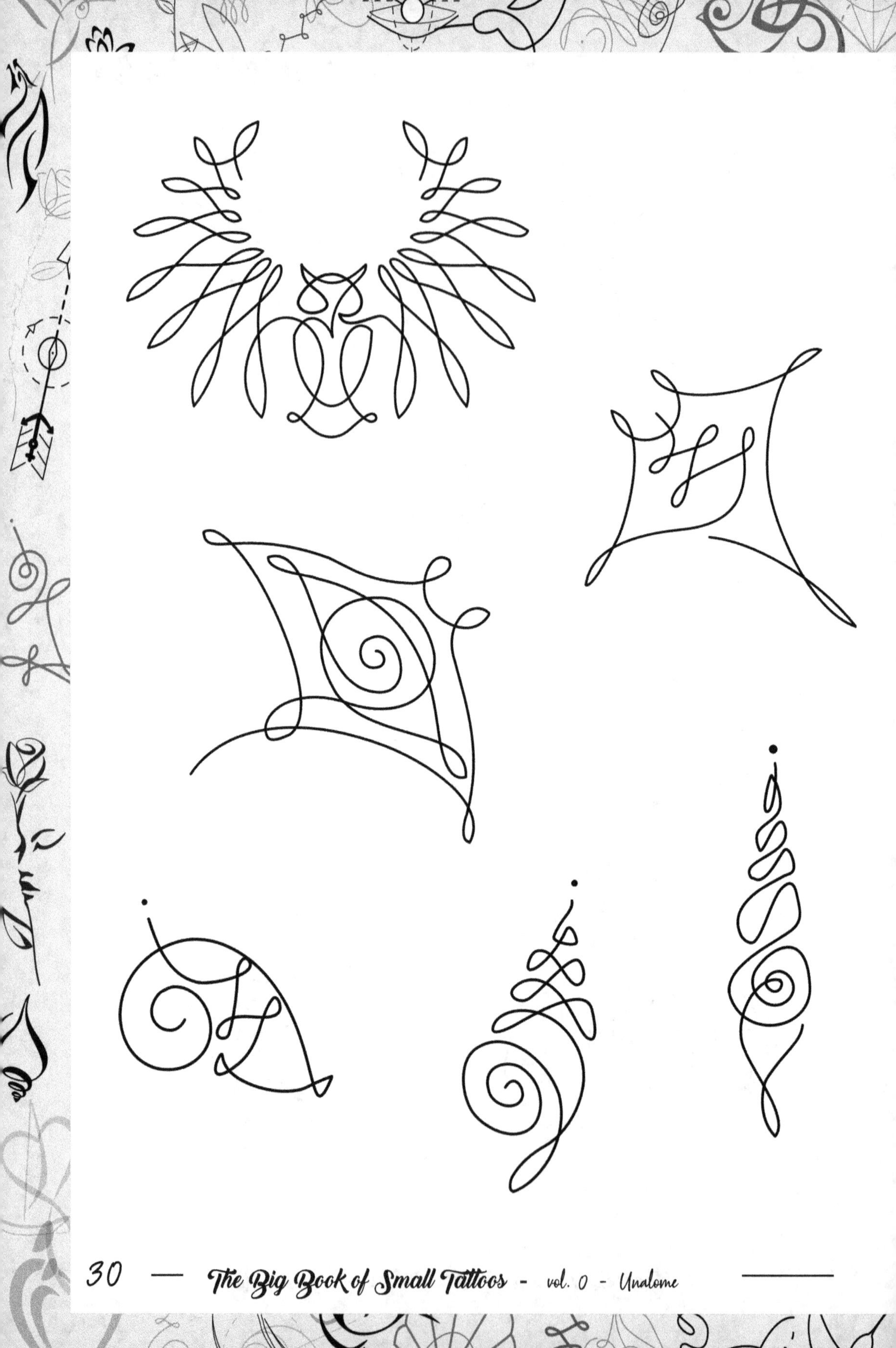

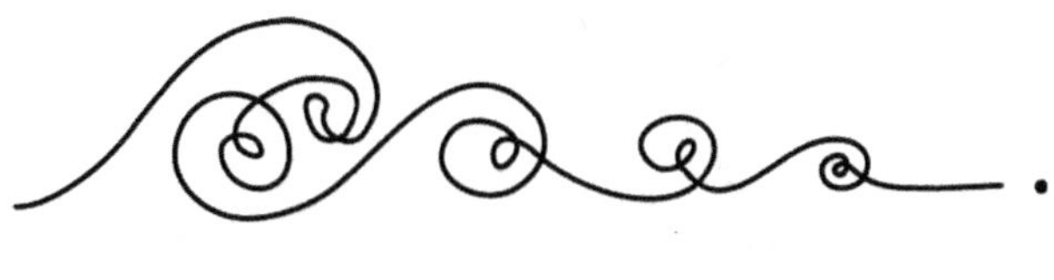

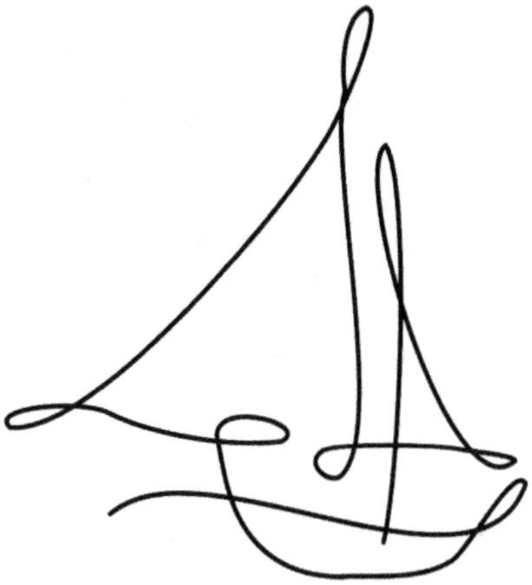

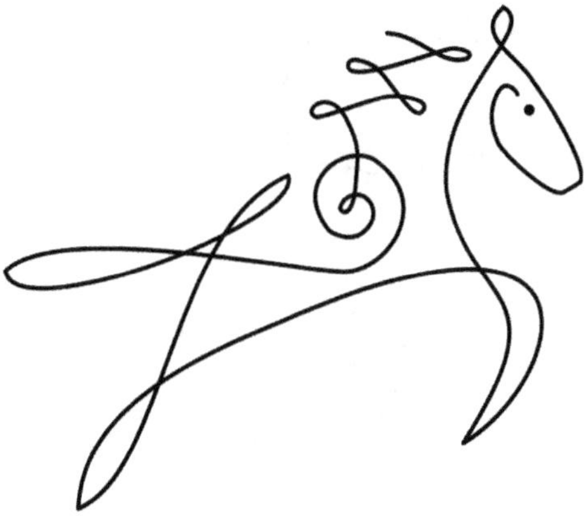

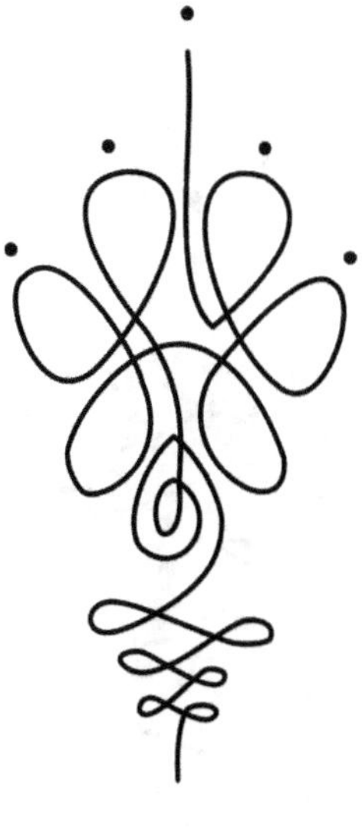

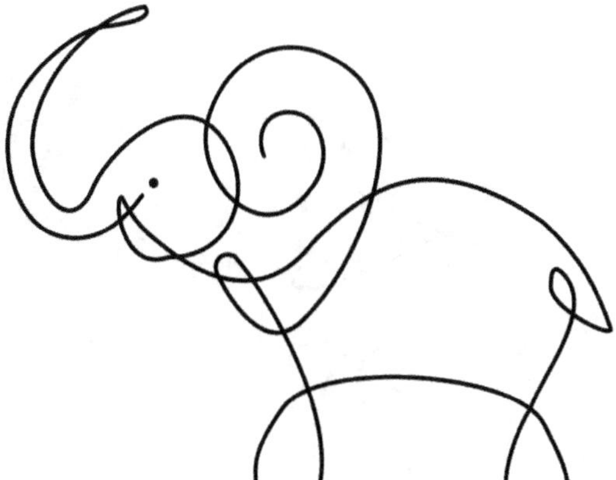

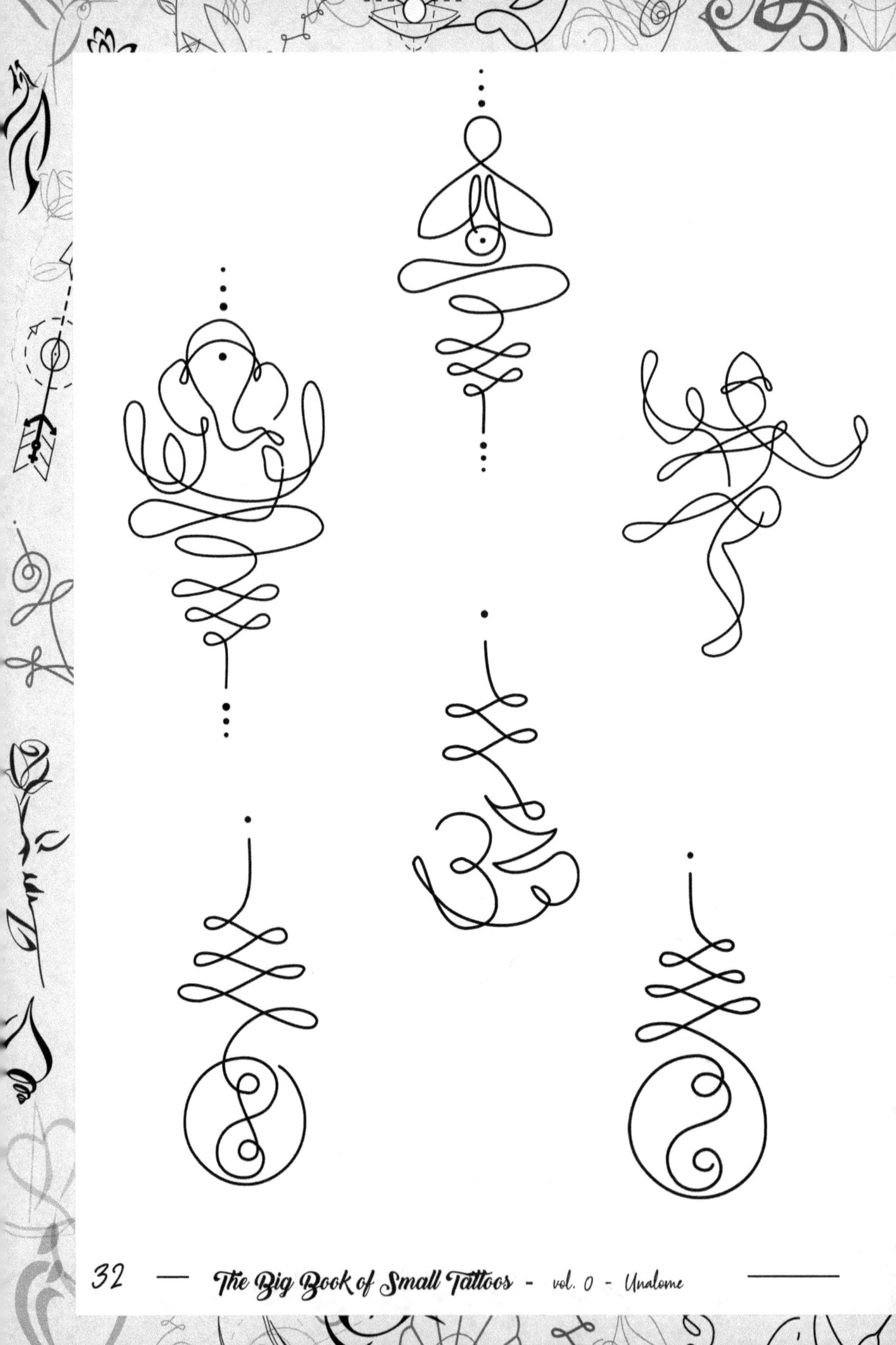

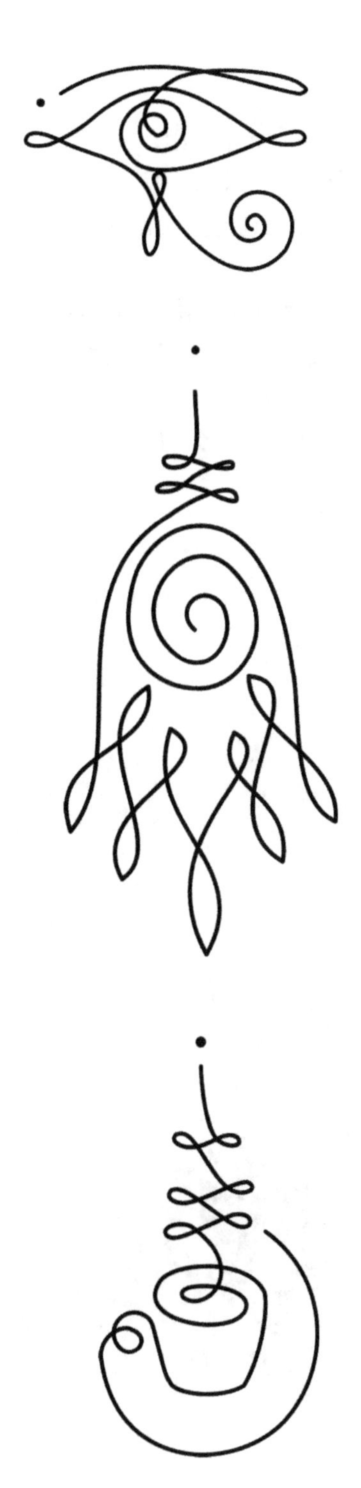

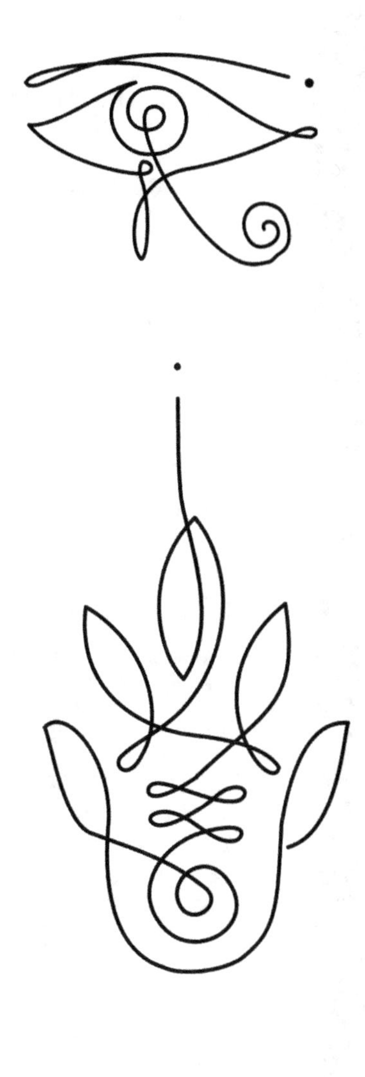

All the designs in the books in this series have never been published before; this is a great opportunity to have a tattoo that's one of a kind.

Each small tattoo can be personalized with just a few minor changes, like adding an element, changing the thickness of its lines, or joining two or more designs together.

Adding colors is another great way to personalize them: watercolor style is a perfect match, and it guarantees that there will never be two designs looking the same.

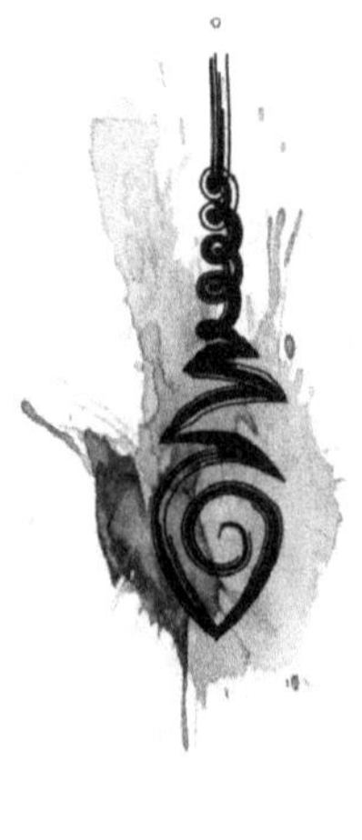

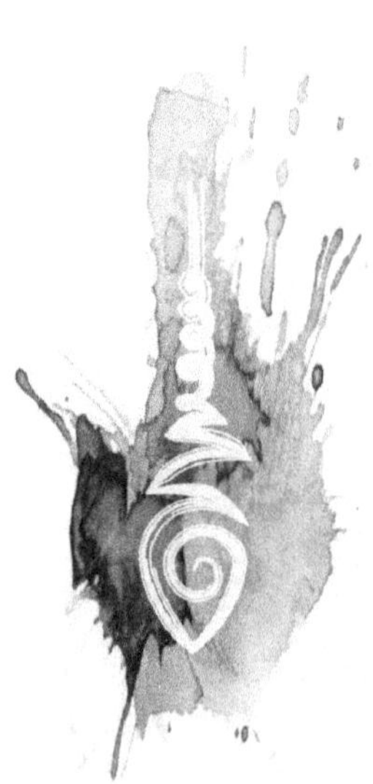

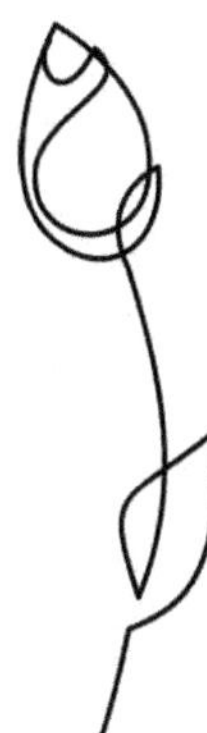

The simplest modification is to thicken some of the lines. It gives more strength and character to a delicate design.

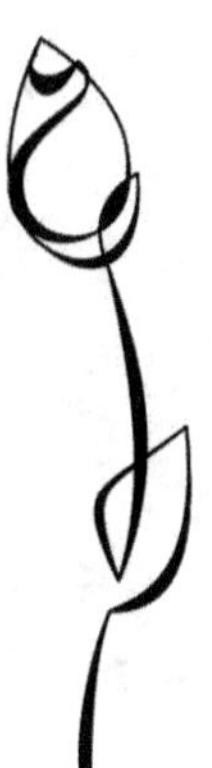

You can also decide to add a shadow to the tattoo, to give it three-dimensionality, or draw it as if it was brush painted. These are all easy ways to make it personal without needing to change the basic symbol.

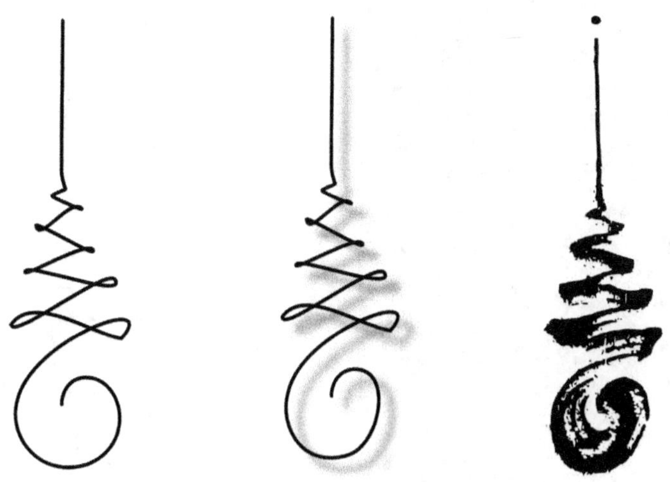

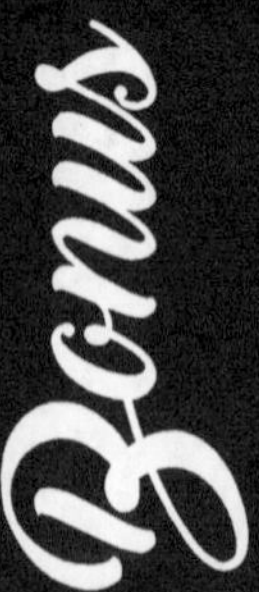

Bonus

All the designs in this bonus section were custom made by TattooTribes for specific persons and therefore should not be used.
   They have been included in addition to the 100+ original ones in this book to inspire you further and to give you even more ideas for creating your perfect tattoo.
   To read their meanings and see more of them, visit www.tattootribes.com

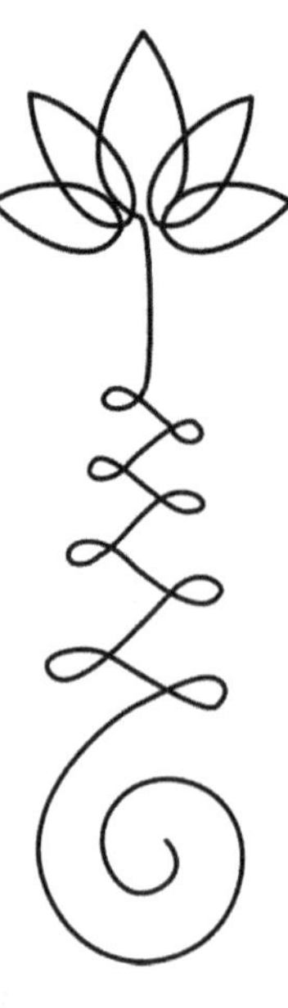

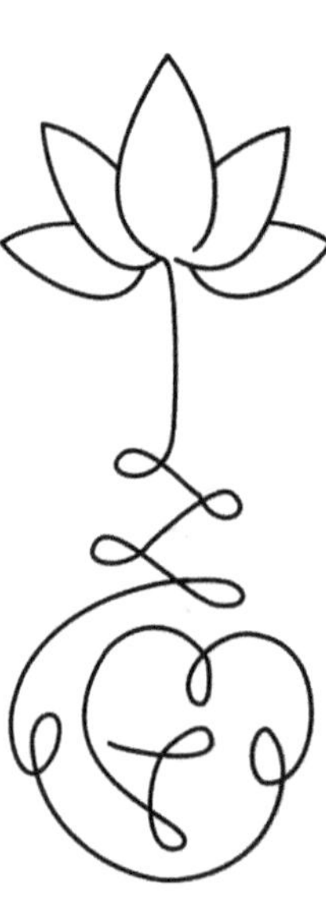

C + A + B

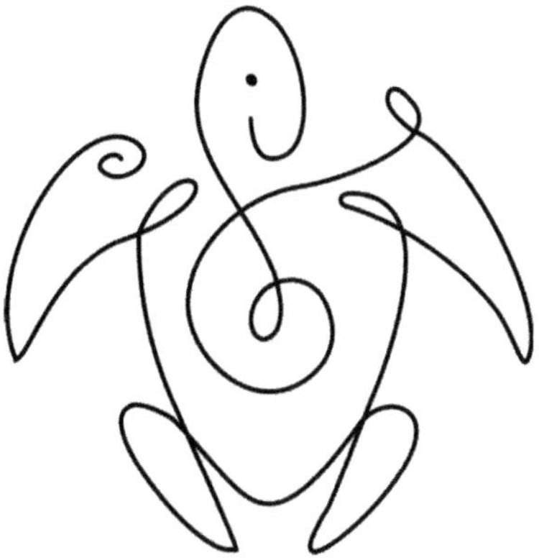

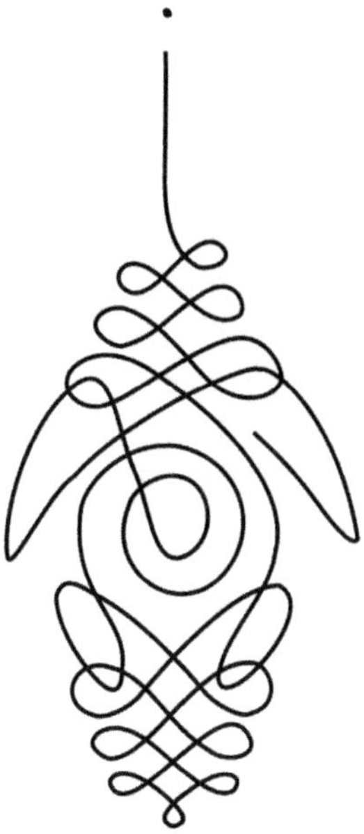

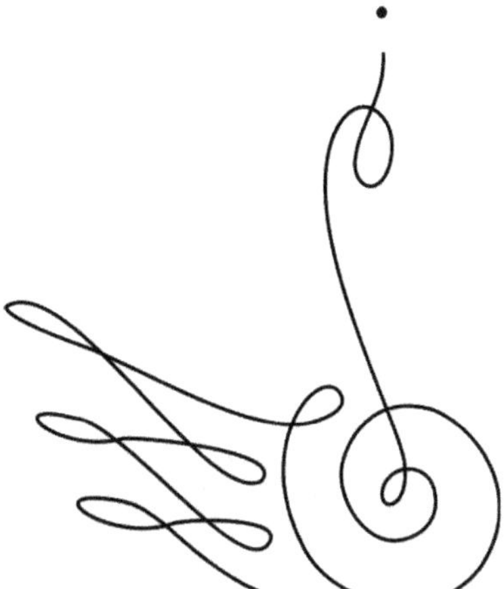

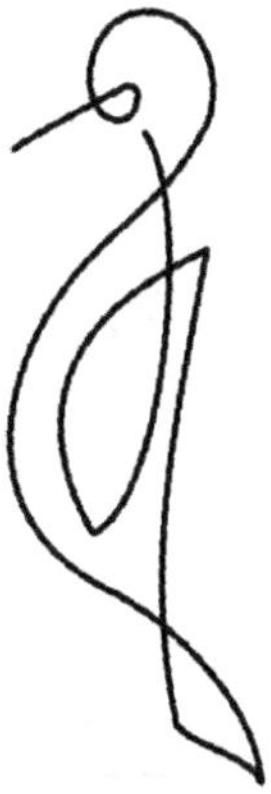

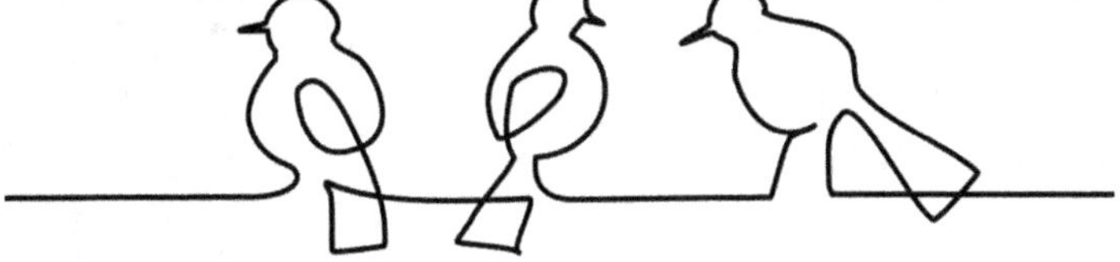

EXTRA BONUS

Follow the QR code on your phone to suggest new themes you'd like to see in one of the upcoming books in this series, and if your suggestion makes it into a book, you'll get a FREE copy of it!

https://www.small-tattoo-ideas.com/suggest.html  

In the same series:

The Big Book of Small Tattoos - Vol. 1 (2019)
400+ Original Small Tattoos for Women and Men
Whether you are approaching tattoos for the first time and want to start small, or
you're a longtime fan and only have just that tiny little spot left, you will appreciate
this book and its philosophy: **small & meaningful**.

More books from TattooTribes:

The Polynesian Tattoo Handbook (2011)
Practical Guide to Creating Meaningful Polynesian Tattoos
Learn Polynesian tattoos and their symbolism. 250+ pages with symbols, their
meanings, their placement on the body, case studies, and step-by-step tattoo
creation, basic elements, and reusable designs.

Polynesian Tattoo Designs (2014)
Vol.1 - Ocean Legacy
A large-format book collecting all 93 Polynesian-styled tattoo designs from design
books numbers 1, 2, 3, and 4, each one accompanied by its stencil: Mantas,
Turtles, Sharks, and Sealife.

The Polynesian Tattoo Handbook, Vol. 2 (2018)
*An In-Depth Study of Polynesian Tattoos and of Their Foundational
Symbols*
Unpacking the five main Polynesian styles: Samoan, Marquesan, Tahitian,
Hawaiian, and Maori. 206 pages, 550+ illustrations, 400+ symbols and variants.

Polynesian Tattoos (2018)
42 Modern Tribal Designs to Color and Explore
A coloring book for adults featuring 42 original tattoos, each one accompanied by
a description of its meanings.

TattooTribes.com
2021